Mysterious Signs Of The Torah Revealed In GENESIS

Publisher
B'nai Noach Torah Institute, LLC,
Post Office Box 14
Cedar Hill, Missouri 63016
First Edition 2012

Mysterious Signs Of The Torah Revealed In GENESIS

Mysterious Signs Of The Torah Revealed In GENESIS

DEDICATED

When I was down you were there
When I needed a friend to listen and share
You were the one to care

When it was difficult and I felt despair
A voice would say, 'I am aware.'
I am here to heal, help and repair

When darkness burdened you would declare,
With me intensely, Shema Yisroel in prayer.'
For this and more I am thankful you are there.

A wife of accomplishment is rare…
Upon you I heavily rely… you are there
Love you bestow on me I cannot compare…

So I want to thank you for all your take care,
Thank you dear little flower of blossom alair,
Kah Nah Naw Har Raw, you make us a pair.

Akiva Gamliel

Mysterious Signs Of The Torah Revealed In GENESIS

Mysteries Of Ha Torah Revealed In GENESIS

Table of Contents

DEDICATED..5
FORWARD..9
PREFACE..13
ACKNOWLEDGEMENTSPix Cam...........................15
GEMATRIA CHART..19
The Revealed Light..21
    Chapter 1..21
Come Into My House..29
    Chapter 2..29
Influence of the Letter Chof In Avraham's Life..........37
    Chapter 3..37
Observing the Protection of the Taryag Mitzvot.........47
    Chapter 4..47
The Mystical Triangle..53
    Chapter 5..53
Mystical Struggles...61
    Chapter 6..61
Contact with the Creator...69
    Chapter 7..69
Yaakov's Mystical Staff..79
    Chapter 8..79
Realizing Our Creator in Every Action......................91
    Chapter 9..91
Osnat, A Praiseworthy Wife.....................................103
    Chapter 10..103
Gematria Footprints of Yoseif..................................111

Chapter 11 111
Learning to Live with Adversity 123
Chapter 12 123
The Seven Laws 137
Chapter 13 137
Glossary Index 143
Torah References 165
ABOUT THE AUTHOR 169

Mysterious Signs Of The Torah Revealed In GENESIS

Mysterious Signs Of The Torah Revealed In GENESIS

FORWARD

I have known many teachers over the years, some are well known, some are not. One thing I know about the author of this book is that he strives to live what he teaches. Dr. Akiva Gamliel has always required references for any work submitted to him. He follows those rules himself and documents all his work. This book is chocked full of information that most of us have never seen. In this book you will find pearls, nuggets of information that up until this time have been left to Jewish scholars. For those who understand the many nuances of Hebrew, discovering these hidden treasures is easy. Yet I know it was not like this for Dr. Akiva Gamliel. At the age of 40, like the great Rabbi Akiva, he did not know even the Aleph Bet, i.e. the Hebrew Alphabet. He applied himself through study for many years. He speaks fondly of those days when he learned with 'his teachers' at the Rabbi's table at Yeshiva Toras Chaim during morning breakfast. Since those days Dr. Akiva Gamliel has grown a great deal. He would say, 'It's not enough'. During those years Dr. Akiva

Mysterious Signs Of The Torah Revealed In GENESIS

Gamliel began studying by invitation. He was invited to learn several evenings a week with a young Rabbi in an old old trailer in a cow field. Much has changed since then. The young Rabbi at that time was the Director of the Division of Community Services for Yeshiva Toras Chaim Outreach Center. Rabbi, Yaakov Meyer is now the head Rabbi of Aish HaTorah, a large Orthodox Congregation and school in Greenwood Village, Colorado.

Back in those early days, Dr. Akiva Gamliel would learn 30 minutes each morning after prayers and before breakfast, with Rabbi Dovid Nussbaum. He is a scholarly Bais Medrash Teacher at Yeshiva Toras Chaim. He is also the son in law of Rosh Ha Yeshiva's Rabbi Yitzchock Wasserman

Dr. Akiva Gamliel learned with Rabbi Mordechai Twerski of the Orthodox Congregation Tri Sulom / The Resh Mem Kehilas Beis Yaakov and worked in the Pesach Matzah factory and as a moshgiach.

Dr. Akiva Gamliel also learned with Rabbi Yisroel Engel of Denver Chabad who is now the Rabbi of Bais Menachem in Denver and also the head of Colorado Chabad.

Mysterious Signs Of The Torah Revealed In GENESIS

Dr. Akiva Gamliel's credentials are many. Besides authoring thousands of web pages on the study of the Torah he also teaches on a weekly basis to hundreds of students through out the world via internet.

Dr. Akiva Gamliel does his own translations. Many of the translations of the Bible that are available to English readers are somewhat inaccurate as any translation would be. He strives to provide a full understanding of the text he is writing about. He also spends hours each day in prayer and study which is why I believe you will find answers in this book that you will not find anywhere else. Most of us can use a little help peeling back the layers and uncovering the mysteries of Bereisheit. This book is for anyone who believes that the Torah is like an undiscovered country just waiting to be explored more deeply. As you read and study this book you will find truth if you are truly seeking it So let's begin this journey.

Mysterious Signs Of The Torah Revealed In GENESIS

Mysterious Signs Of The Torah Revealed In GENESIS

PREFACE

The Bible is a Book of many mysteries. Within the Bible are the Five Books of Ha Torah, Genesis, Exodus, Leviticus, Numbers and Deuteronomy. The conundrum within Ha Torah is different than within the rest of the Bible. Why? What is hidden in Ha Torah has many quandaries. Within Ha Torah there is a system of Hebrew Letters which each have a numerical value. The numerical values reveal many interesting, perplexing, bewildering and mystifying relationships within the Hebrew Letters, Words, Phrases etc. of Ha Torah that I discuss in this book. Some call this numerology. Others call this Gematria. I call this a study of אותות Oh Toht / Signs.

For more than two decades during my daily Torah study I recorded various Oh Toht / Signs as they were unveiled to me as well as those revealed to other scholars of much greater stature. As I study Ha Torah The Creator Reveals a glimpse of the hidden. The Gematria in this book came from exploration. I was created with a curious mind. It is a

Mysterious Signs Of The Torah Revealed In GENESIS

special honor to share from these Gematrias - these Signs in this book. May the Creator be praised!

A great deal of Oh Toht is about relationships. Hebrew Letters share ties with numbers that unveil many principled secrets if one knows what to look for. No matter how much information is known about certain Hebrew Word or numbers only a small portion is known in comparison to the entire picture. I have been gathering, compiling and organizing for many years kah nah nah haw raw. Many years can pass between one discovery to another which forms a bridge between two discoveries. Revelations are the product of many bridges. Enclosed in this book are some of these special relationships.

There is a special sweetness in sharing a Torah Gematria / Sign during a wonderful Shabbat or High Holy Day meal.

ACKNOWLEDGEMENTS

My parents have gone on to the next life, may they rest in peace. Momma would have deeply enjoyed the discussion in this book. She was a detail oriented Bible Scholar. We shared many interesting, fiery intense discussions that warm my soul to this day. Momma reminded me more than once, 'Buddy don't give God the hot end of the poker.' Thank you Momma.

Daddy was an orphan from the age of five. He worked fervently to make a place in this world for Momma, my brothers and his grandkids. Life was challenging for him until the very end when he departed in his sleep on Erev Sabbath / Friday night. He would tell associates that he graduated from the school of hard knocks. Daddy's favorite statement was, 'Keep on keeping on.' Thank you Daddy.

My Former Father – In – law, may he rest in peace, used to say, 'Don't give me roses when I'm dead. Give me roses while I'm alive [when I can enjoy them.] His favorite statement was about tithing. He would tell his congregants, You don't pick your groceries up at this store then walk across the street and pay for them at another store.'

Mysterious Signs Of The Torah Revealed In GENESIS

I acknowledge that my Step – Mother – In – Law is truly a kind Spiritual Lady. I am blessed thank God! Kah Nah Naw Haw Raw. Katie listens to every concern with patience and then offers encouragement and prayer. She cares about other people. She is a most excellent example for others to follow. May she be blessed with good health and a long life... Thank you Katie.

The greatest acknowledgement that one can make is to say and to mean the Lord God is my Creator. He is King of this Universe and of all that exists. He is Holy and His Name is Holy. God Willing someday in the future I will join the many individuals already in the heavens with our Creator and express my many appreciations to them. In this book I share a few stories about them.

My acknowledgement to my wife is that a praiseworthy wife is so rare. It is very difficult to reach such a lofty level. Thank you for trying, Dad Belk said, "trying counts!' He was right. Please be understanding regarding those rare occasions when you may not have reached the highest level of Aishet Chayil. After all look who you are married to. I made it a challenge even though many times it was not intentional. Thank you for trying!!

My acknowledgement to my brothers is to seek the

truth that you do not know and when you find it do not be afraid to embrace it. King David said that the Torah [Law] of the Lord is perfect, Psalms 19.8. Why would God want to replace the Torah?

A very important acknowledgement is to my two sons and two step sons. REGARDLESS of what anyone tells you, each of you are required to honor your mother and your father every hour of your life. I wish that I had been a much better example for you to observe and follow. Never cease to teach your children to *Honor their father and their mother so that their days may be long upon the land which the Lord our God Gives them... [regardless of their age]*, Shemot / Exodus 20.12.

Someday my grandchildren will read this book when they are older and curious and want to know more about their Zadie. To them I acknowledge that אמת Emet / Truth will stand on its own. Look at the Letters. Ever letter of Truth stands on it own. Each Letter of Truth has two legs and a foundation. Truth will stand up to all questions. Never be afraid to ask many questions. The opposite of Emet is a שקר sheker, a lie. Look at the Letters. Each letter of a sheker has no foundation and only one leg to stand on. Our Sages Teach a sheker will fall before Emet..

Mysterious Signs Of The Torah Revealed In GENESIS

Mysterious Signs Of The Torah Revealed In GENESIS

GEMATRIA CHART					
Aleph	א	1			
Bet	ב	2			
Gimmel	ג	3			
Dalet	ד	4			
Hey	ה	5			
Vav	ו	6			
Zayin	ז	7			
Chet	ח	8			
Tet	ט	9			
Yud	י	10			
Chof	כ	20	Final	ך	500
Lamid	ל	30			
Mem	מ	40	Final	ם	600
Nun	נ	50	Final	ן	700
Samech	ס	60			
Ayin	ע	70			
Pey	פ	80	Final	ף	800
Tzzadi	צ	90		ץ	900
Quf	ק	100			
Reish	ר	200			
Shin	ש	300			
Tav	ת	400			

Mysterious Signs Of The Torah Revealed In GENESIS

The Revealed Light
Chapter 1

Bereisheit Bereisheit
Bereisheit / Genesis 1.1 – 6.8

וַיַּרְא אֱלֹהִים אֶת־הָאוֹר כִּי־טוֹב וַיַּבְדֵּל
אֱלֹהִים בֵּין הָאוֹר וּבֵין הַחֹשֶׁךְ׃

And He, God saw that [everything from the letter Aleph to the letter Tav] of the Light was good. And He, God differentiated between the Light and between the Darkness. **Bereisheit / Genesis 1.4**

Mysterious Signs Of The Torah Revealed In GENESIS

וַיַּרְא אֱלֹהִים אֶת־הָאוֹר כִּי־טוֹב וַיַּבְדֵּל אֱלֹהִים בֵּין הָאוֹר וּבֵין הַחֹשֶׁךְ :

In Bereisheit / Genesis 1.4, we observe the Words את האור Eht - Haw Ohr. This means *Everything from the Letter Aleph to the Letter Tav of the Light.*

Let's discuss the word את Eht. The letter Aleph is the first letter of the Hebrew Aleph Bet / Alpha Bet. The letter Tav is the last letter of the Hebrew Aleph Bet. In the example that follows the letter א [Aleph] is on the Right and the letter ת [Tav] is on the left. Remember Hebrew is read from the right to the left.

אבגדהוזחטיכלמנסעפצקרשת

The words את האור Eht - Haw Ohr are the beginning of Spirituality and Judaism as we know them. Mystically, the Gematria of Eht - Haw Ohr represents the 613 Commands of Ha Torah. In Judaism we teach that our Creator gave B'nei Yisroel / the Children of Israel, 613 Commands to observe. The 613 Commands of Ha Torah are often referred to as the תריג Taryag Mitzvot. The 613 Commands are recorded in Ha Torah which is Genesis, Exodus, Leviticus, Numbers and

Deuteronomy. There is an excellent book, <u>The Taryag Mitzvos</u> written by Rabbi A. Y. Kahan that lists and briefly explains each of the 613 Commands of Ha Torah. It's easy reading, educational and enjoyable.

Each letter of the Hebrew Aleph Bet is represented by a number. The combined letters of the words את האור Eht - Haw Ohr equal 613. The 613 of the words את האור Eht - Haw are representative of the 613 Commands our Creator gave to B'nei Yisroel.

$$613 = 200\text{ר} + 6\text{ו} + 1\text{א} + 5\text{ה} \quad 400\text{ת} + 1\text{א}$$

We understand the Light was good. Mystically we learn that the 613 Commands from Ha Torah are good. Mystically we also learn that the light flows through observance of the 613 Commands of Ha Torah.

Now we move to the last three words of Bereisheit 1.4, האור ובין החשך Haw Ohr - Oo Vayn - Ha Choh Shehk meaning [God differentiated between] *the Light and between the darkness*. What differentiates between the light and the darkness? Ha Torah differentiates between the light and the

Mysterious Signs Of The Torah Revealed In GENESIS

darkness. How do we know this?

613 = ר20 ש300 ח8 ה5 ן50 י10 ב2 ו6 ר200 611א ה5

We understand that God differentiated between the Light and between the darkness. Mystically we understand that it is the 613 Commands of Ha Torah that differentiates between Light and darkness. On Yom Echad / Day One neither the sun or moon were created. Think about how Light and darkness existed. Neither the Light or the darkness existed as most people realize it today. Mystically we can now understand that in Passuk / Verse three that God said, Let [My] Light be revealed. The Commands of Ha Torah divide the Creator's Revealed Light from the darkness.

I began by saying, the words את האור Eht - Haw Ohr are the beginning of Spirituality and Judaism. We observe that Judaism is established through Ha Torah and through observance of the 613 Commands of Ha Torah. Now we should ask, what about Spirituality? What is Spirituality? Spirituality as I define it is the observances that Adam Ha Reshon / Adam the first man and Chavah [Eve] Ha Reshonah / Chavah the first lady followed. Mystically we can understand God revealed His Light through the 613 Commands of Ha Torah. The 613 Commands are for B'nei Yisroel. What about Adam

Mysterious Signs Of The Torah Revealed In GENESIS

and Chavah? Our Sages teach that our Creator gave Seven Commands to humankind. The Seven Commands are first noted in Bereisheit 2.16. They are not revealed in English translations. Most Hebrew translations do not mention them when commenting on Bereisheit 2.16. Yet, this is where Torah Spirituality originates from. Spirituality is the observance of the original Seven Commands that the Lord God commanded in Bereisheit 2.16. Our sages teach that the Seven Commands expand into sixty-six Commands. The Seven Commands may expand into more than sixty-six Commands. If you would like to learn more about the original Seven Commands please visit bnti.us or 7commands.com. I discuss them there.

And He, God said, Let [My] light be [revealed] and there was Light. Bereisheit 1.3

We can Mystically see the 7 Commands in another Gematria. This Gematria discipline is known as Gematria Mispar Katan. This is where ONLY the first number is counted. Here are a few examples. A 10 is 1, 100 is 1, 90 is 9, 60 is 6 and 400 is 4. Using Gematria Mispar Katan we can mystically see the 7 Command for Spiritualists in the word יהי [אור] Let

[My] Light be [revealed].

Normal Gematria of יהי [אור] Yih He [Ohr], Let [My] Light be [revealed] is 25. Gematria Mispar Katan of יהי [אור] Yih He [Ohr] is 7.

25 = 10י 5ה 10י

7 = 1י 5ה 1י

One may ask why it is proper to use Gematria Mispar Katan instead of Normal Gematria. Katan means smaller. 7 Commands of Ha Torah are smaller than 613 Commands of Ha Torah.

We understand that God said, Let [My] Light be [revealed] and there was Light. Mystically we can now see that the precursor to revealing His Light was the 7 Commands.

Neither Judaism nor Spirituality discount personal experiences. A Christian felt the need to share with me how she received healing. I told her we do not discount personal experiences. She still had to tell me every detail of her healing. I was acquainted with her sickness, its length and her full recovery. Blessed is HaShem! After she took all this time to explain in detail her healing she concluded, 'And I prayed in Jesus' name.'

I replied, So what? She repeated her claim as if I had not heard her the first time or did not understand. Again I replied, So what? She was flabbergasted! She wanted to know how I could say such a thing. I explained that many people of many different religions have had healings, powerful answers to prayer and incredible experiences. She understood this might be possible. I went on! Tehillim / Psalms 145.18,19 says that our blessed Creator hears the cry of those that call upon Him. HaShem / the Lord says that *it is the cry that I hear*. Dear ones, many humans of different religious / persuasions cry out to HaShem using the name of Jesus or of Mary or a Saint Peter or of a religious leader. HaShem hears the cry! So please keep in mind that even though it is wrong to use a medium to approach our Creator He understands more than word or language or name can express. We pray to our Creator with our understanding. We pray to our Creator with the Light that has been revealed to us. The Lord knows the cry of His Creation. He hears their cry just as a mother knows the cry of her children. We come to our Creator from the most twisted and wretched situations in life. Thank God

Mysterious Signs Of The Torah Revealed In GENESIS

He hears and responds to us. Our Creator responds to honest, sincere cries of his creation! Blessed is His Name!

There is an important point that we miss in Sefer Yonah / Jonah. The men aboard the vessel with Yonah each cried out to their own god. Were their prayers answered? Yes! Did the gods answer their prayers? NO! The Lord God heard their cries and answered them. HaShem God heard the cries of His creation. The men aboard that vessel cried out in accordance with the Light that was revealed to them. Later these same men forsook their gods and cried out to HaShem. Why? They cried out according to the new Light imparted to them by Yonah. See Yonah 1

Mysterious Signs Of The Torah Revealed In GENESIS

Come Into My House
Chapter 2

Bereisheit Noach
Bereisheit / Genesis 6.9 – 11.32

וַיֹּאמֶר יְהוָה לְנֹחַ בֹּא־אַתָּה
וְכָל־בֵּיתְךָ אֶל־**הַתֵּבָה** כִּי־אֹתְךָ
רָאִיתִי צַדִּיק לְפָנַי בַּדּוֹר הַזֶּה:

And He, HaShem / the Lord said to Noach you go and your household into the Ark For I have seen you are righteous before me in this generation. Bereisheit 7.1

Mysterious Signs Of The Torah Revealed In GENESIS

The wind was fierce! The waves seemed like they were a hundred feet high as they swept across our ship from the bow to the fantail. Our ship rocked from starboard to port, shaking ferociously as we encountered wave after wave after wave crashing and smashing against us! Large six by six wooden deck planks were ripped away by the waves with little effort. Our ship's boarding and exiting ladder was viciously torn from its place and carried off into the depths of the ocean. Shipmates were tossed to and fro as well as the ship's cargo. The enormous screw that propelled our ship was often lifted up out of the water by huge waves as the fo'c'sle at the other end of the ship dipped deep into an ocean valley. At times one could stand with their face only a few feet from the deck due to the incredible motion of the ship. Where I worked pots, pans, spoons, whips and other galley utensils went flying through the air as our ship sunk into one of these vast ocean valleys created by the intense storm.

This was one of four typhoons I experienced at sea. A typhoon is an unnerving, soul shaking experience that can last for days at a time. A typhoon is a storm in the region of the Indian ocean and the western Pacific ocean with violent wind like that of a hurricane. The motion of vast ocean waves and clouds mixed with torrential rain is unspeakable. Knowing this I cannot imagine what it would be like to experience a worldwide decimating flood as in the days of Noach!!

A flood is such a violent force capable of moving everything in its path. Its path is one of absolute destruction! Where can one run? Where can one hide? Where can one find security? Where can one find safety? Where can one find shelter?

Thousands of years ago in Noach's flood there was only one place of safety. The ark was the only place of shelter!!

The Gematria of התבה Ha Tay Vaw is 412. This is also the Gematria of בית Bah Yeet, meaning house. In this instance, Ha Tay Vaw represents a special house, a house above the world. Ha Tay Vaw represents the house that floats on water. Ha Tay Vaw represents the house of safety! Ha Tay Vaw represents the house of salvation! Each time HaShem makes reference to Ha Tay Vaw He is actually offering comfort and reassurance to the eight people who will endure the world's horrible destruction.

Mysterious Signs Of The Torah Revealed In GENESIS

This is clearly established once Noach completes Ha Tay Vaw. *HaShem said to Noach you go and your household into the Ark, For I have seen you are righteous before me in this generation.* In other words, HaShem invited Noach and his household into His House which would shelter them from the destruction of the world. In realizing this we observe HaShem's care for the residents of the ark as mentioned in the twenty-two occurrences of Ha Tay Vaw. We observe their acceptance of HaShem's invitation to security within the ark...

Ha Tay Vaw - The Ark

412 = 5ה 2ב 400ת 5ה

Bayit - House

412 = 400ת 10י 2ב

Again, there is no way to describe what the eight survivors experienced but it does help to know that HaShem prepared the survivors, guided them and assisted them in reestablishing after the flood. This is defined in the meaning of bayit house. In other words the ark was their transitional house, from their house in the old world to their house in the new world. House implies a building, a structure, a place of gathering, a place of living, a place of learning and more. House implies security like home, a place to come home to after the world's destruction...

Holy reader, think of the gargantuan transition from old to new... Everything... every bayit, every house, would have to be reestablished after the destruction... by just eight people. These eight people had to be learned to reestablish a House of Education. They had to be horticulturists... the earth has just experienced the most incredible physical transition. Oceans are now mountains. Seas are plains. Mountains are oceans. The water canopy covering earth has been removed. The hemisphere has changed. Temperatures are no longer constantly hovering around 72 degrees. Parts of Mother Earth are now very cold while other parts are extremely hot and humid... a house of horticulture had to be built. Many houses had to be built. Let your mind expand on this thought... the baker's house... the grocer's house... the house of prayer...

Ha Tay Vaw represented the transfer from the bayit of the past to the bayit of the future. It was the vessel, the house, that transported what HaShem ordered to be brought from the past to the future... animals...books... tools... seeds... clothing... So Ha

Mysterious Signs Of The Torah Revealed In GENESIS

Tay Vaw was the bridge house from the past to the future...

Life has a bridge between man and God. The directions for building this bridge is Ha Torah. The bridge is constructed through observance of Torah! The bridge of Torah assists us in our transformation from a life of sin to a life of holiness. God willing the bad things in our life are left in the old world. Those things are not transported on Ha Tay Vaw. On Rosh Hashanah we leave the old house and transport Spiritually to a new house in a new year. Our old sins and mistakes were left behind with the old house to be destroyed. On Rosh HaShanah we enter a our new house. This is our second week of Torah study and observance. We are transferring all the good things carried with us in Ha Tay Vaw from our old house to our new House of Torah that we are constructing for this year. May this year's house be a very good house!!

Two little boys were discussing Chanoch / Enoch. The first little boy asks the other, *Do you know why God took Chanoch?*

The second responds, *No.*

The first little boy continues, *Well, one day Chanoch was walking with God. God turned to Chanoch and said, 'Chanoch, you're closer to My home than yours. Why don't you come home with Me?' So Chanoch went home with the Creator.*

HaShem God prepared a special house for Noach and his family to protect them from the storm of destruction. They were safe in their house, the Ark. There are times when each of us need to feel safe. We want to feel protected. We want to feel close to our Creator as Chanoch. We want to feel like we have a bridge from this side of life to the other. We can if we draw close to the Creator. Moshe wrote, *The [individual] who dwells in the shelter of the Supreme One will abide under the protection of Shadai... With His wings He will cover you and beneath His wings, you will find refuge: His truth is a shield, a full shield.* Tehillim / Psalms 91.1,4.

Mysterious Signs Of The Torah Revealed In GENESIS

Mysterious Signs Of The Torah Revealed In GENESIS

Influence of the Letter Chof In Avraham's Life
Chapter 3

Bereisheit Lech Lecha
Bereisheit / Genesis 12.1 -17.27

וַיֹּאמֶר יְהוָה אֶל־אַבְרָם לֶךְ־לְךָ
מֵאַרְצְךָ וּמִמּוֹלַדְתְּךָ וּמִבֵּית אָבִיךָ
אֶל־הָאָרֶץ אֲשֶׁר אַרְאֶךָּ:

And HaShem said to Avram, [first] 'Go' [second['Get Out' from your land, and from your birthplace, and [away] from your father's house, [and go] to the land I will show you.
Bereisheit 12.1

Mysterious Signs Of The Torah Revealed In GENESIS

Terach and Avram fled Ur Kasdim / the fiery furnace for Charan after Avram's delivery by HaShem. They were journeying to Canaan.

There is a dispute as to where Avram was when he was first commanded to leave his land. I believe the command to leave his land originated in Ur Bavel. Sefer HaYashar / The Book of Jasher records that Avram lived with Noach for a month after Ur Kasdim. *Avram said to his father, "...Do you not think that it would be safer for all of us to leave this vicinity and go to Canaan? ...So accompany me and we shall then serve [God] and abandon the emptiness of these surroundings." ...They left Ur Bavel and made their way to Canaan.* Sefer HaYashar (Hoboken, NJ: KTAV Publishing House, Inc., 1993) p.31 As a side note: Noach lived until 2006 F.C. From Creation. Avraham was born in 1948 F.C. See Dr. Akiva Gamliel's 16 Month Calender - Yahrzeit Dates of Ha Torah (Denver, CO, Debar Publishing 2009)

Avram was in Canaan, returned to [Charan], and left for good five years afterwards with his entire family. Heninrich W. Guggenheimer, Seder Olam {A Jason Aronson Book, Lanham, Maryland, Rowman & Littlefield Publishers, Inc. 2005) p

Avram lived in Ur Kasdim with his father Terach, his brother Haran and Sarai. Haran died in the fires of Ur Kasdim. It was there that he received the command Lech {Go!}. In response to this command, Avram and his father Terach made plans to journey to Canaan as noted in Sefer Hayashar. This is the first part of Bereisheit 12.1, *get away from your country*. They set out on this journey, but for some reason they stopped in Charan and settled there. This is the second part of Bereisheit 12.1, *get away from your relatives*. They left Ur Kasdim, but they had not arrived in Canaan.

Avram intended to go to Canaan to settle. According to our sages he visited Canaan when he was 70 years of age but he did not stay there. He returned to Charan. It was from Charan that the third part of Bereisheit 12.1 occurred, *get away from your fathers house...* So half of his journey remained unfinished. It was to this unfinished business that HaShem spoke to Avram a second time, represented by the Lecha 'Get out!'. If Lech meaning 'Go' or 'Leave' was not adequate then a stronger command Lecha 'Get out!' was necessary.

Originally Avram and Terach were traveling together. Originally they appeared to have the same goals. That changed when they arrived in Charan. Terach settled there. He was content. Avram desired to continue on to Canaan, the original goal. Avram was torn! Should he stay with his father? Should he leave his father? This was a difficult struggle for this righteous man. That is why a second command was required.

Go [from Ur Kasdim]! Get out [of Charan]!! Get away from your birthplace! And get away from your father's house!

Ha Torah makes it very clear that Terach had set up his household in Charan. Ha Torah records HaShem's words, "Get away from your father's house!" Yet we should notice that Avram was not told to leave his house in Charan. He was commanded, "Get away from your birthplace!" That is because Avram had not established his house in Charan. Yet Ha Torah records that *they settled there [in Charan]*. Bereisheit 11.31 Avram settled there with the intention of continuing on to Canaan. Terach settled there with the intention of dying there. This is why Ha Torah records Terach's death at that time even though he was only 145 years of age. Ha Torah records Terach's death to be at the age of 205, sixty years later. Why?

In Gematria the letter Chof is 20. Notice that the end of each statement ends with the letter Chof as shown in the beginning of this article. The Chof equals 20. Avram was instructed by HaShem to:

Go away from your land.

מארצך

Go away from your birthplace.

וממולדתך

Go away from your father's house.

ומבית אביך

The three Chof's equal 20 x 3 = 60.

Remember Terach, father of Avram, chose to stay in Charan and die there which is exactly what he did 60 years before he was buried. In other words, each Chof represents Avram's choice to obey HaShem and Terach's choice to disobey HaShem. The Gematria Mispar Katan reduces the Chof from 20 to just 2. The two represents the choice to obey and the choice to disobey. It also represents agreement as in "How can two walk together except they be agreed?" It represents the agreement that both Terach and Avram should have continued with, but did not. It represents the agreement that Avram entered into with HaShem.

This is because he faltered from his original plan of going on to Canaan. He lost his glimpse of light. His vision of Canaan grew dim. Our sages say with regard to Terach that *'the wicked are called dead even while they are alive.'* Terach was on the path to repentance, but became entangled along the way and returned to his evil ways of idol making in Charan. Avram could not persuade his father to change or to go on. Why? Evil relatives in Charan influenced Terach. This is why Avram was commanded by HaShem to *Get away from your father's house!* Actually it was more like Get away from your father's EVIL house. Get away from your father's EVIL INFLUENCE... Get away from the EVIL influence of your relatives...

Years ago when I used to smoke cigars and chew tobacco, a relative brought a pair of tiny blue jeans to me.. pointing to the back rear pocket. There was this round crease from a tobacco can. My youngest son was learning a bad habit from his father. He was carrying a tobacco can... The relative said to me, "See what you are teaching your son?" Dear reader, I cried out to God in my heart, "*Please give me the strength to stop... stop chewing tobacco, stop smoking cigars... stop teaching my son poor habits.*" One morning shortly after this prayer I woke up with the confidence that 'Today'... that this morning was the day to quit. Thank God, that was my day.

Holy reader, every work... every action... every thought... every act of thoughtlessness generates an impression and an image. What would we like our legacy to be? What do we want to pass on?

Moshe passed Ha Torah on... What do we want to pass along?

I listened to the boys mom.. I stopped smoking cigars and chewing tobacco. I want to be a good influence on my children and grandchildren. I did not want my actions to hinder my children. I wanted my children to be close by. I did not want them to feel the need to get away from dad because he was toxic.

In addition לך לך Lech Lecha is the Gematria of 100. The letter Chof when spelled equals 100. This Gematria discipline is known as Gematria Miluy.

The letter כף Chof

Mysterious Signs Of The Torah Revealed In GENESIS

100 = 80 ף 20 כ

Avraham was 100 years old when Yitzchok was born. Bereisheit 21.5

The letter Chof is formed by a heavenly Zayin and an earthly Zayin. Notice the picture of the letter Chof in the Book <u>The Wisdom of the Hebrew Alphabet</u>. 'The holiness on earth represented by the Zayin pointing towards the heavens typifies a hand lifted in praise towards God. The holiness of the heavens, represented by the Zayin pointing to earth, typifies a hand extended to earth, scattering blessings to mankind. When the Zayin of Heaven and the Zayin of earth join they form one hand, the Chof, twenty. Life on earth should be like life in the heavens. The Chof represents the word 'like' when attached to the front of a word.' Rabbi Michael Munk The Wisdom In The Hebrew Alphabet Mesorah Publications, Brooklyn, N.Y. 1990), p. 133

Please notice the Chof that follows.

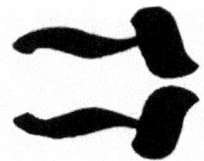

14 = 7ז + 7ז

Mysterious Signs Of The Torah Revealed In GENESIS

Mysterious Signs Of The Torah Revealed In GENESIS

Mysterious Signs Of The Torah Revealed In GENESIS

Observing the Protection of the Taryag Mitzvot
Chapter 4

Bereisheit Vayera
Bereisheit / Genesis 18.1 -22.24

וַיְהִי אַחַר הַדְּבָרִים הָאֵלֶּה וְהָאֱלֹהִים נִסָּה אֶת־אַבְרָהָם וַיֹּאמֶר אֵלָיו אַבְרָהָם וַיֹּאמֶר הִנֵּנִי :

And it happened after the words, the oath and then God tested everything from the letter Aleph to the letter Tav of Avraham, and He said to Avraham, and he [Avraham answered], Here I am. Bereisheit 22.1

Mysterious Signs Of The Torah Revealed In GENESIS

The fifth, sixth and seventh words equal the Gematria 613. והאלהים נסה את Vih Haw El-Him - Nee Saw - Eht - Avraham {And then God tested [everything from the letter Aleph to the letter Tav] of Avraham}. This reminds us when we are going through tests to remember to observe the 613 Commands of Ha Torah. It is difficult to stand when going through tests. It is difficult to observe the 613 Commands of Ha Torah when going through tests. One feels like they need to be protected, like they need to be shielded. Just as sheep are gathered into a corral we need to be gathered into the corral of the Great Shepherd, HaShem. The boundaries of the fence are the 613 Commands of Ha Torah

613 Mitzvot / Commands of Ha Torah
Vih Haw El-him - Nee Saw - Eht - Avraham
613 = 400ת 1א   5ה 60ס 50נ   40ם 10י 5ה 30ל 1א   5ה 6ו

Protective Fence Pen or Corral

613= 400ת 6ו 200ר 4ד 3ג

In being tested, Avraham opened the door for his descendants to receive the 613 Mitzvahs of Torah. This is evident to us. Yet our emphasis is on the great value of successfully passing a test. The purpose of the Akeidah was to prove that there was strength in the agreement between God and Avraham. It was to place the agreement between God and Avraham on trial. Avraham was tested to see if he would obey God's Command. We are also tested to see if we will obey God's commands. Now, we are not commanded to sacrifice our children as Avraham was, Thank God! Yet we are tested. When we are tested, our test can reach the same proportion as Avraham. We can and do experience what Avraham experienced even though we are not commanded to sacrifice our only son. How can this be?

Avraham faced his test relying on what God had promised him. We share in the promises of our father Avraham. Each generation from Avraham until now shares in the Covenant between Gd and B'nei Yisroel. Our children and grandchildren and great grandchildren share in our agreement. Yet like Avraham we must be tested to demonstrate the dedication, honor and strength of our agreement with God. The Samech represents the continuous agreement and the continuous tests. Like the letter Mem the Samech is a continuous circle. The Jewish people are like that circle. The Gematria for Hah Law Caw {law, rule tradition} is the Gematria of 60. We use the term Hah Law Caw to designate the way in

Mysterious Signs Of The Torah Revealed In GENESIS

which we should walk / live. Mystically this is exemplified in the test of Avraham, that is the way to follow God's Commands.

Gematria Mispar Katan:
Vih Haw El-him - Nee Saw - Eht -Avraham
והאלים נסה את אברהם
6ה1א5ל3י1ם4 5נ6ס5ה א1ת4 א1ב2ר2ה5ם4 = 60

Hah Law Caw - The Law The Way to go in
ה5 ל30 כ20 ה5 = 60

Even though our father Avraham passed his test, we sometimes fail our tests. The story of the ten spies who brought back an evil report is an example of our failing tests. We, Kal Yisroel failed our test. In our cycle of life we will have more opportunities to pass or fail tests. So we need to prepare. We need to connect with God and to connect with the Truth of Torah.

I knew a man, Raphael. His life was not easy. Its all a matter of how one faces and deals with issues. Raphael's family descended from Germany. He served as an American solider in W.W.II. He was decorated for his bravery. He contacted malaria and nearly died. In his twenties he was a drinker. He overcame this problem, exhibiting great self control throughout the last forty years of his life. In forty plus years of close contact I did not observe anger, loshon hora or unfaithfulness to HaShem. Raphael was honest in business. He was not perfect but he lived a righteous life!

Raphael did not attend a Jewish day school or a Yeshiva, yet he studied often. Even with all his learning efforts he was far from being a Torah scholar. Yet that did not stop his great Chessed / Kindness or great Rachmanoot / Compassion / Mercy to the indigent, the sick and the elderly. He frequently visited them and helped them. Was Raphael tested? Yes! Did he pass life's tests? Yes!

He had little to leave for his children even though he worked very hard all his life. He owned a small two bedroom house, one car, one suit, one jacket and several pairs of slacks. Yet he was one of the happiest men I have had the honor of knowing. Why? His focus was not on himself. His focus was not on what he owned. Raphael's focus was on helping others.

Mysterious Signs Of The Torah Revealed In GENESIS

The Mystical Triangle
Chapter 5

Bereisheit Chayei Sarah
Bereisheit / Genesis 23.1 – 25.18

וַיִּהְיוּ חַיֵּי **שָׂרָה** מֵאָה שָׁנָה וְעֶשְׂרִים
שָׁנָה וְשֶׁבַע שָׁנִים שְׁנֵי חַיֵּי שָׂרָה:

And it was the lifetime of Sarah, one hundred years, and twenty years and seven years, [These were the] years of Sarah's life.
Bereisheit 23.1

Mysterious Signs Of The Torah Revealed In GENESIS

Parshat Chayei Sarah begins with the words ויהיו חיי שרה Vah Yeeh Yoo- Chah Yay Sarah, meaning, and it was the lifetime of Sarah. One should inquire, what was the lifetime of Sarah? In so doing they would find these three words reveal rich treasures. The Gematria of Vah Yeeh Yoo - Chah Yay Sarah is 570. Why is 570 so special? There are many Gematrias of 570.

This was the lifetime of Sarah
570 = 5ה200ר300ש 10י10י8ח 6ו10י5ה10י6ו

Shema [Yisroel]
570 = 50ן10י70ע 40ם40מ 50ן10י300ש

To Be Rich
570 = 200ר 300ש 70ע

The number 570 represents the lifetime of Sarah our Matriarch and richness. Sarah Emeinu / our mother's, lifetime was one of great wealth. Her life was filled with richness.

Shlomo Ha Melech / King Soloman said, *An accomplished wife who can find? Far beyond [rich] pearls is her value.* Mishlei / Proverbs 31.10

Mysterious Signs Of The Torah Revealed In GENESIS

Our sages Teach Sarah's tent was Sarah's Temple. Sarah Emeinue brought Holiness into her home. *Her home was no ordinary tent. It had extraordinary qualities: A cloud [the Shekinah] of Holiness [resting over it], doors which proclaimed their openness to all passers-by, a blessing in her dough, a Sabbath lamp that remained lit all week* long. These miracles were not Abraham's doing; they ceased with Sarah's death. Rabbi Meir Zlotowitz and Rabbi Nosson Scherman, The Artscroll Tanach Series - Bereisheit Vol. I(b) (Brooklyn, New York: Mesorah Publications, Ltd. 3rd Impression, 1989), p 832

The Shekinah over Sarah's Home represented that this was a holy home. God's Presence Rested over it. The home was protected! There were special blessings of satisfaction in Sarah's dough that flowed out to the entire community. Just as the bread of the Bet HaMikdosh / the Holy Temple Brought prosperity and abundance to B'nei Yisroel, so did Sarah's bread. Sarah's Esau candles represented spiritual growth that would begin with each Erev Esau and last all week. *When Sarah died all of these vanished. With Sara's death the Cloud of Glory over the tent vanished, the blessing in the dough ceased, and the candle that had burnt in the tent from one Erev Sabbath to the next was extinguished.* Rabbi Moshe Weissman, The Midrash Says (Brooklyn, New York: Benei Yakov Publications 1980), p. 210

Mysterious Signs Of The Torah Revealed In GENESIS

When Sarah lived a cloud covered her tent; when she died, the cloud left. When Rebekah came, the cloud returned. When Sarah lived, the doors to her tent were wide open. When Sarah died the liberal giving ceased. When Rebekah came, the liberal giving returned. When Sarah lived, there was blessing upon her dough. The Sabbath candle / oil burn from the evening of the Sabbath until the evening of the following Sabbath. When Sarah died, these ceased. When Rebekah came they returned.
Rabbi Dr. H. Freedman, Midrash Rabba Genesis II (New York, NY: The Soncino Press 1983) p 538

Within Gematria there is a particular mysticism known as Gematria Miluy in which one totals all the normal Gematria Letters in a word or phrase. Such is the instance with the Word Shema {Hear}. This reveals the wealth of Sarah's prophecy. Notice the seventeenth Hebrew Word of Bereisheit 21.12. It is [שמע] Shih Mah. Rashi points out that it is from this Passuk of Ha Torah that we learn Avraham was inferior to Sarah with regard to prophecy. Rabbi Avrohom Davis / Rabbi Avrohom Kleinkaufman, The Metsudah Chumash / Rashi (Hoboken, NJ: KTAV Publishing House, Inc. 1993) p221

The entire spelling for שמה Shema is:

570 = 50נ 10י 70ע   40ם 40מ   50נ 10י 300ש

Mysterious Signs Of The Torah Revealed In GENESIS

Gematria for the Miluy of Shema is 570. Here we observe the wealth of Sarah's prophecy.

A Tenth / To Tithe
570 = 200ר 300ש 70ע

The life of Sarah Emeinu was a lifetime of paying her tenth to Shem the son of Noach {Noah} who was a Kohen {a Priest} of the Most High Alm-ghty and who was also known as Malki Tzedek / King of Righteousness. Rabbi Yisrael Isser Zvi Herczeg, The Sapirstein Edition Rashi Bereisheit / Genesis {Brooklyn, New York: Mesorah Publications, Ltd. First Edition 10th impression 2007}, p 139

How do we know this? Shem was the head of the tribe that Avraham belonged to. As head of the tribe he was a priest. Who does one pay their tithes to? A Kohan {a Priest} of the Most High God! Today in place of a Priest we pay tithes to good organizations and good causes. Yet the point is that we are supposed to pay tithes. עשר Aw Sar means to tithe to pay a tenth. The Gematria of עשר Aw Sar is 570. Sarah Emeinu paid tithes all her lifetime! She set a good example for all her children to follow! There are many other Gematrias that relate the wealth of Sarah Emeinu.
Sarah's Gate:

Mysterious Signs Of The Torah Revealed In GENESIS

570 = 200ר 70ע 300ש
Shlomo Ha Melech writes in Mishlei / Proverbs 31.31 *Let her be praised in the* בשערים *Vah Shih Aw Ree {gates} by her very own deeds!* בשערים Vah Shih Aw Ree is plural for שער Shah Ahr {gate}. שער Shah Ahr is the Gematria 570. We know that Sarah Emeinu's home was holy! Holiness began at the gate entrance to Sarah's tent area.

Sarah Emeinu kept evil away from her gate / door.

570 = 70ע 300ש 200ר
Remember God Instructed Kayin / Cain *Sin is crouching at your door*, Bereisheit 4.7. We must keep the רשע Raw Shaw evil at a distance. The Message God Was Giving to Kayin is the same message for all of us. Keep the Raw Shaw outside of our Temple! Be aware that the Raw Shaw is waiting outside our Temple to try and pounce on us, God Forbid! Our mother Sarah, was successful in keeping the evil checked at the gate entrance. The Gematria for Raw Shaw is 570.

Sarah kept her evil Inclination in Check.

570 = 70ע 200ר 200ר 90צ 10י
Sarah kept her יצר רע Yay Tzehr Raw in check. Our sages teach that Sarah was perfect! The only

way Sarah Emeinu could be perfect was to have a firm control on her evil inclination! This she did! This is all a part of the wealth of Sarah.

Like an Eagle:

570 = 200ר 300ש 50נ 20כ

[Sarah] *soared on wings like eagle,* Isaiah 40.31. Cih Neh Shehr, *Like an eagle she stirred her nest hovering over her young,* Devarim Deuteronomy 32.11. Sarah was all of these Gematrias in one.

Then Sarah prayed! She began her day with prayer.

מודה אני לפניך מלך חי וקים

296 =   20ך 50נ 80פ 30ל   10י 50נ 1א   5ה 4ד 6ו 40מ

264 = 40ם 10י 100ק 6ו   10י 8ח 20ך 30ל 40מ

570 = 296 + 264

And the vast wealth of Sarah goes on and on. Avraham in part was great because of Sarah!

Mysterious Signs Of The Torah Revealed In GENESIS

Name	Age	Reference
Avraham	100	Bereisheit 17.17;21.5
Sarah	90	Bereisheit 17.17

There was a ten year difference between Avraham & Sarah.

Name	Age / Date	Reference
Sarah	100	Bereisheit 23.1
Yoseif	110	Bereisheit 50.22
Sarah	20	Bereisheit 23.1
Yoseif	30*	Bereisheit 41.46

*Stood before Pharaoh

Sarah	7	Bereisheit 23.1
Yoseif	17**	Bereisheit 37.2

**Sold into Slavery

It is interesting to note the ten year match between dates in our Mother Sarah's life and Yoseif son of Yaakov.

May every lady merit to be like Sarah and may every husband merit a wife like Sarah! May every couple merit a son like Yoseif.

Mysterious Signs Of The Torah Revealed In GENESIS

Mystical Struggles
Chapter 6

Bereisheit Toldot
Bereisheit / Genesis 25.19 - 28.9

וַיִּ**תְ**רֹצֲצוּ הַבָּנִים בְּקִרְבָּהּ וַתֹּאמֶר אִם־כֵּן
לָמָּה זֶּה אָנֹכִי וַתֵּלֶךְ לִדְרֹשׁ אֶת־יְהוָה׃

וַיֹּאמֶר יְהוָה לָהּ שְׁנֵי גיים [גוֹיִם] בְּבִטְנֵךְ
וּשְׁנֵי לְאֻמִּים מִמֵּעַיִךְ יִפָּרֵדוּ וּלְאֹם מִלְאֹם
יֶאֱמָץ וְרַב יַעֲבֹד צָעִיר׃

And they crushed [and bruised and struggled] the sons inside her, and when this happened she questioned why is this happening to me? And she went to inquire from Aleph to Tav about this from HaShem. Bereisheit 25.22

And said HaShem to her, 'Two nations are in your womb and two peoples will separate from within you and to one people will be fullness [and great] boldness and the great will serve the junior.' Bereisheit 25.23

61

Mysterious Signs Of The Torah Revealed In GENESIS

Our Parshat begins with Yitzchok pleading to HaShem for children. His wife Rivkah is barren... Yitzchok is sixty years of age. Rivkah is twenty-three years old when she conceives, see Bereisheit 25.26. When Yitzchok took Rivkah as his wife he was forty and she was three, see Bereisheit 25.16. KJV uses the word damsel. See Strong's reference # 5291, (a girl from infancy to adolescence). This is based upon Bereisheit 23.1. Sarah is 127, Avraham is 137 and Yitzchok is 37. It is immediately after the Akeidah that Avraham 'was informed [by HaShem] that his son's mate had been born, in accordance with the verse, Behold Milcah, she [has borne] etc.' Rabbi Dr. H. Freedman, <u>Midrash Rabba</u> (New York, NY: The Soncino Press 1983) - Midrash Rabbah writes, *Tamar was the daughter of Shem.* p 504

Yitzchok and Rivkah did not consummate their marriage until she was twelve or thirteen. Ten years passed. Then Yitzchok prays for his wife to have children, see Bereisheit 25.21.

The girl.. והנערה Vih Hah Nah Ah Raw Rivkah was only three. See Bereisheit 24.16. Her mother and brother refer to Rivkah as לנערה Lah Hah Nah Ah Raw, the girl. See Bereisheit 24.57. They felt she was attached to her present family. They felt she was too young to leave home even though boys and girls then, were much different than they are today. They were more developed. They were more intelligent. They worked from a very young age. To verify this consider, Yaakov's children. All in all five references in Ha Torah refer to Rivkah as a young girl.

Yaakov's oldest child Reuben, who was born after Yaakov had worked for Laban for seven years, kept the flock for his father, which was a three-day journey away. Ha Torah states, *He gave them [the sheep] to his sons,* Bereisheit 30.35. Ha Torah states, *He [Yaakov] placed them a three days journey [away],* Bereisheit 30.36. How old were his sons when this happened? This was after Yaakov had served Laban for 14 years. He served seven years for Leah and seven years for Rachel, then he served six years for his cattle. {Bereisheit 31.41} This means that Reuben was no older than six years three months old when he began keeping his father's flocks with his brothers. Reuben was born to Yaakov after Yaakov had worked for seven years. Yaakov then worked an additional seven years. It was during the first year of that second seven-year period that Yaakov's first wife, Leah, gave birth. This was the birth of Reuben. Now all the other brothers were much younger. The second son, Shimon, was around five. Levi, the third son, was around four. Judah was close to three. It was at this point that Rachel gave Bilhah to Yaakov. So, dear reader, we see that Ha Torah establishes the age of children who worked a full day, and who were responsible to be much younger than children today.

Now this proves that the age of Rivkah, three, when she married Yitzchok was not out of the question. It is well within the realm of possibility!! Yet this is why they sent Devorah, Rivkah's nurse, along with her.

Interesting letters are added to several of the words in the first Passuk / Verse. This is not by mistake. I have noted the letters. The Yud represents the intensity of the struggle between Esau and Yaakov. The Tav in Vah Yeet Roh Tzah Tzoo represents that this fighting in the womb of Rivkah was a sign. The Tav in Vah Toh Mehr represents another sign. Rivkah spoke out loud to her sons. *Why are you fighting?* Like a mother would say to her children, *Why are you fighting / hurting your brother?* Yet this was very puzzling to Rivkah.

Our sages state that when Rivkah would pass by the doorways of Torah study at the school of Shem and Evier, Yaakov would rush to come out, and when

Mysterious Signs Of The Torah Revealed In GENESIS

Rivkah would pass by houses of idol worship Esau would rush to come out. Can you imagine how Rivkah must have felt?

Let's examine this a little closer. Notice the phrase, שני גוים בבפנך Shih Nay - Goh Yeem - Bih Veet Naych {Two nations are in your womb} Within these three words there are two unique acrostics. An acrostic is the composition in which certain letters in a line form a word or words. In the first acrostic notice the first Letter, i.e. on the right. In the second acrostic notice the last Letter on the left.

The first acrostic is from the first letter of each of the three words below from the phrase **Shih Nay - Goh Yeem - Bih Veet Naych**. This is noted in the first example. The second acrostic is taken from the last letter of the last two words of the same phrase. The second acrostic follows the first as Yaakov followed Esau in birth. This acrostic is taken from the last letter of the last two words of the same phrase. I noted this by making these letters darker. Esau was the first born. The first acrostic refers to him.

שגב = בבפנך גוים שני

Saw Gahv {to be high, mighty, strong,

Mysterious Signs Of The Torah Revealed In GENESIS

extolled, sublime}.

305 = 2ב 3ג 300ש

שני גוים בבפנך

[Final Mem]   ם = מ   [Normal Mem]

מך
Mawch {poor, humble}

60 = 20ך 40מ

The second acrostic describes Yaakov the second born son, the son who fled from his brother. Yaakov was the son who for twenty years was the poor son. From a lesson in a course {Torah 203} at B'nai Noach Torah Institute, LLC entitled Yaakov's Staff we take the following quote which discusses Yaakov's poverty: *'Our sages teach that when Yaakov fled his father Yitzchok's home, Elifaz, the son of Esau, went after him {Yaakov} and overtook him. Elifaz was ordered by his evil father Esau to murder his Uncle Yaakov. Yet Elifaz was*

Mysterious Signs Of The Torah Revealed In GENESIS

raised by his grandfather Yitzchok. Elifaz did not want to disobey his father's order to kill his Uncle Yaakov, even though he realized it was an evil order. Elifaz recognized this responsibility to his father, yet he also recognized his responsibility to do righteousness... When he overtook his Uncle Yaakov he explained his predicament. His Uncle Yaakov helped him sort things out.

...Yaakov's counsel to his nephew was to take everything that he [Yaakov] had with him because a poor man is considered dead. So Elifaz heeded his Uncle Yaakov's counsel and took everything but Yaakov's clothes and staff.

So from the same three word phrase Shih Nay - Goh Yeem - Bih Veet Naych {Two nations are in your womb} we have the acrostic of Saw Gahv {to be high, mighty, strong, extolled, sublime} representing Esau and the acrostic of Mawch {poor, humble} representing Yaakov. The Gematria of שגב Saw Gahv is 305. The Gematria of מך Mawch is 60.

The Gematria 305 through Mysticism describes the actions and intent of Esau in the word להרע Lih Haw Rah {to hurt, harm; to do evil} which is what Ha

Mysterious Signs Of The Torah Revealed In GENESIS

Torah states Esau intended to do to his brother Yaakov. *Esau said in his heart, 'The days of mourning for my father are approaching. I will then kill everything from Aleph to Tav of my brother, Yaakov,'* Bereisheit 27.41. Esau's evil intention was to make it seem as if Yaakov had never been born or existed.

להרע Lih Haw Rah {to hurt, harm; to do evil}
305 = 70ע 200ר 5ה 30ל

הלכה Ha Law Chawh {law, rule, tradition}
60 = 5ה 20כ 30ל 5ה

In the Gematria 60 we see reverence for God and reverence for His Commands in Ha Torah in the word הלכה **Hah Law Chawh** {law, rule, tradition}. It was Yaakov who loved to study Hah Law Chawh, according to our sages. Yaakov who loved to dwell in tents of learning. Yaakov learned with Shem, the righteous son of Noach, and with Eiver, the righteous great grandson of Shem.

So among these two nations we see Esau, the high, mighty and strong one, subdued by Yaakov, the humble student of Ha Torah!

Mysterious Signs Of The Torah Revealed In GENESIS

Contact with the Creator
Chapter 7

Bereisheit Vayeitzei
Bereisheit / Genesis 28.10 - 32.3

וַיֹּאמֶר יְהוָה אֶל־יַעֲקֹב שׁוּב אֶל־אֶרֶץ
אֲבוֹתֶיךָ וּלְמוֹלַדְתֶּךָ וְאֶהְיֶה עִמָּךְ׃

And He, HaShem said to Yaakov return to [the] land of your father and to your birthplace and I will be with you. Bereisheit 31.3

Mysterious Signs Of The Torah Revealed In GENESIS

When an individual reads the Bible they maybe lead to believe that our Creator speaks often with humankind. An examination of Biblical history does not support this position. Even though a good amount of Ha Torah shares the revelations, dreams, visions, and communications between our Creator and humankind they are over a long period of time. Ha Torah records Adam's contact with God as just five times within Ha Torah over 930 years. About once every 186 years or just five times on the sixth day and then never again...

1. Adam the man
Bereisheit 1.28-30
Bereisheit 2.15-17
Bereisheit 2.20
Bereisheit 2.21,22
Bereisheit 3.9-24

2. Chavah / Eve
Chavah, Adam's wife, had only one contact with God in her entire life...
Bereisheit 3.13-16

3. Kayin
Kayin, the brother of Hevel and son of Adam and Chava, had just two contacts with God during the

seven generations {spanning hundreds of years} of his life...
Bereisheit 4.6,7
Bereisheit 4.9-16

Hevel who was murdered by Kayin had no recorded contact with
God...

Seth, the third recorded son of Adam and Chava, had no recorded contact with God...

Enoch walked with God for 300 years but no direct contact is indicated...

From Creation forward to the time of the Flood, these are the only people Ha Torah records that our Creator communicated with. Ha Torah records that just three people - Adam, Chava and Kayin - had contact with God during the period from Adam up to Noach. Contact with God was not an everyday event. In other words, there are eight recorded contacts with God from creation to Noach. There were eight recorded contacts from Creation to Kayin's murder of Hevel, then no recorded contacts for over 1,600 years.

Mysterious Signs Of The Torah Revealed In GENESIS

Now if one were to venture outside of Ha Torah to search for human contact with our Creator *Sefer a Yashar* records a few additional communications between HaShem and humankind. *Sefer Ha Yasher* records that a Malach / an Angel visited Chanoch / Enoch. Sefer HaYashar (Hoboken, NJ: KTAV Publishing House, Inc., 1993) p.12 Later Sefer Ha Yasher records that God told Methushelach and Noach to '...proclaim to all the world as follows: *"Thus says [God]. Repent of your evil ways and He will change the decree He has made against you. Obediently, both these men proclaimed this warning to all. This they did day after day, but people refused to take heed. Now [God] set a deadline of one hundred and twenty years. This gave them further opportunity to repent, and [God] then would likewise withdraw His plan of destruction...'* Sefer HaYashar (Hoboken, NJ: KTAV Publishing House, Inc., 1993) p.16

At the time of the Flood, the earth's population was millions, maybe even billions. *Sefer Ha Yashar* reports that over 700,000 people gathered around the Ark after the door was shut and the flood began. Sefer HaYashar (Hoboken, NJ: KTAV Publishing House, Inc., 1993) p.18
Sefer Ha Yashar is mentioned twice in the Bible. KJV call Sefer HaYashar the Book of Jasher. It is quoted in Joshua 10.13 and 2 Samuel 1.18.

4. Noach had contact with God
Bereisheit 6.13-21
Bereisheit 7.1-4
Bereisheit 7.16
Bereisheit 8.15
Bereisheit 9.1-17

Contact at Babel and confusion of languages
Bereisheit 11.7-9

5. Abraham had contact with God
Bereisheit 12.1-3
Bereisheit 12.7,8
Bereisheit 12.17
Bereisheit 12.14-17
Bereisheit 15.1-20
Bereisheit 17.1-22
Bereisheit 18.1-33
Bereisheit 21.8
Bereisheit 22.1,2
Bereisheit 22.11-14
Bereisheit 22.15-24

One evening I experienced the type of dream that one wants to continue. I was lost and alone on a very dark night. In the far distance a light twinkled... a light sparkled. After hours of walking towards this light it grew brighter and brighter. It was a beacon light for lost souls, like me... The light was very powerful! It shone in all directions constantly. I wondered while walking towards the light, what is a beacon of light doing in the middle of nowhere?...

Eventually I reached a location not too distant from where the light was shining. It was the tent of Avraham Aveinu {our father} just after his Brit Milah. HaShem's presence was very powerful! The light was a beacon of HaShem in Avraham's tent reaching out into the night. There were no walls to Avraham's tent. Only a cover and corners. In the center of the tent was a prepared table with challah and wine where HaShem's Presence emanated. Avraham restlessly paced back and forth looking off into the night for lost souls... for visitors... for anyone...

This is when my dream ended. This dream reminds me of Avraham's closeness with the Creator. Avraham had close contact with the Creator, yet Avraham's contact with the Creator is a dozen or less times recorded in Ha Torah.

6. Sarah
Bereisheit 18.15

Mysterious Signs Of The Torah Revealed In GENESIS

7. Yitzchok
Bereisheit 22
Bereisheit 26.2-5

8. Rivkah
Bereisheit 25.23

9. Hagar
Bereisheit 16.7
Bereisheit 21.17-21

10. Ishmael
Bereisheit 21.17-21

11. Lot
Bereisheit 19.1-22

Residents of Sodom / Gomorrah
Bereisheit 19.1-29
12. Abimelech
Bereisheit 20.3-8

13. Yaakov
Bereisheit 28.12-15

From Creation to the evening that Yaakov placed his

head upon the stone {which represents a span of 2,185 years}, God spoke through dreams, visions, messengers {angels} and special events like the Flood, Babel and the destruction of Sedom / Amorrah approximately 35 separate times... This is not to say that God did not talk to other people or that every contact is recorded.

The fact is, according to Ha Torah, God spoke to just a few people over a period of thousands of years. God passed judgment on mankind three times. Each time His destructive power was witnessed by millions: at the Flood, at Babel and at the destruction of Sedom / Amorrah.

Now we read that 'HaShem said to Yaakov...' Yaakov is the 13th person that Ha Torah records as being spoken to by the Creator. This is the 36th time in Ha Torah where we observe HaShem having communication with a human or humans. The last time we read of HaShem having communication with a human was 20 years earlier. This time was also with Yaakov. Now after Yaakov's working 20 years... slaving for Lavan, HaShem speaks to Yaakov instructing him to return to his father's house. HaShem speaks to Yaakov this second time in year 2235 from Creation. It was only 187 years before this date that the Creator instructed Yaakov's grandfather Avraham to *'Go!'* for the first time to Eretz Canaan, then again 5 years later to *'Get out!'* *'HaShem said to Avram to "go away from your land and away from your place of birth and away from your father's house...'* Bereisheit 12.1 Now, 182 years later, HaShem is instructing Avraham's grandson to *'return to the land of your fathers and your birthplace.'* Bereisheit 31.3

When HaShem called to Avram in Bereisheit 12.1, Avram was 75 years old. Twenty-five years later Yitzchok was born. Sixty years later Esav and Yaakov were born {25 + 60}. Ninety-seven years later Yaakov was instructed to return to Eretz Canaan. How do we know Yaakov was 97? In Bereisheit 47.9 Yaakov is 130. In Bereisheit 41.46 Yoseif was 30 years old when he stood before Pharaoh. There were 7 years of plenty {Bereisheit 41.29}; that makes Yoseif 37. Then when his father and brothers came to Mitzriam they were into 2 years of famine. {Bereisheit 45.6} That makes Yoseif 39 when his father stood before Pharaoh. So Yaakov was 130 and Yoseif was 39. That means Yaakov was 91 when Yoseif was born. It was then that Yaakov desired to return to his father. His 14 years of service were up. A new agreement was made. See Bereisheit 30.25,26. According to Bereisheit 31.41 Yaakov served Lavan 6 years for his cattle. 91 + 6 = 97 years of age when Yaakov left Lavan. Why is it so important to tie the time between Avram and his grandson Yaakov together? 25+60+97 = 182. Why? Because the Gematria of Yaakov's name is 182.

יעקב Yaakov

182 = 2ב 100ק 70ע 10י

This is quite interesting and special. In essence HaShem is commanding Yaakov to leave his father-in-law, his brothers-in-law, his relatives, their houses and their birthplace and to return to Eretz Canaan 182 years after his grandfather was commanded to go to Eretz Canaan... the Gematria of Yaakov's name. The number 182 is the essence of Yaakov's name and is the passage of time between the father and the grandson entering Eretz Canaan.

Yaakov's Mystical Staff
Chapter 8

Bereisheit Vayishlach
Bereisheit / Genesis 32.4 - 36.43

Bereisheit 32.11

קָטֹנְתִּי מִכֹּל הַחֲסָדִים וּמִכָּל־הָאֱמֶת אֲשֶׁר עָשִׂיתָ אֶת־עַבְדֶּךָ כִּי בְמַקְלִי עָבַרְתִּי אֶת־הַיַּרְדֵּן הַזֶּה וְעַתָּה הָיִיתִי לִשְׁנֵי מַחֲנוֹת:

00I am contracting from all the kindnesses and from all the truth that You appointed from Aleph to Tav for your servant. For with this rod I passed through everything from Aleph to Tav of the Yarden and now this [rod] has turned into two camps. Bereisheit 32.41

Mysterious Signs Of The Torah Revealed In GENESIS

In the previous chapter we discussed the Gematria of Yaakov's name {182} in connection with the time measured between when Avraham was commanded to go to Eretz Canaan and when his grandson Yaakov was commanded to return to Eretz Canaan after 182 years.

Elifaz was Conflicted
From this passuk we especially notice the Gematria of the word במקלי Vi Mahk Lee {with my staff}. As already mentioned Our Sages teach that when Yaakov fled his father Yitzchok's home, Elifaz, the son of Eisov, went after him {Yaakov} and overtook him. Elifaz was ordered by his evil father Eisov to murder his Uncle Yaakov. Yet Elifaz was raised by his grandfather Yitzchok. Elifaz did not want to disobey his father's order to kill his Uncle Yaakov even though he realized it was an evil order. Elifaz recognized this responsibility to his father, yet he also recognized his responsibility to do righteousness! He was conflicted! How could he do both? When he overtook his Uncle Yaakov he explained his predicament. His Uncle Yaakov helped him sort things out.

So many of us are placed in predicaments, conflicting situations. We either have strong allegiances or feel strong emotional obligations to others as well as our responsibility to Ha Torah. This is where Elifaz was... It is a difficult place to be in. So what did he do? He consulted with a Tzaddik. He consulted with Yaakov regarding his predicament. Now Yaakov's counsel to his nephew was to take everything that he [Yaakov] had with him because a poor man is considered dead. So Elifaz heeded his Uncle Yaakov's counsel and took everything but Yaakov's clothes and staff. It is clear that Elifaz did not know the value of his uncle's staff.

See Rabbi Yisrael Isser Zvi Herczeg, The Sapirstein Edition Rashi Bereisheit / Genesis {Brooklyn, New York: Mesorah Publications, Ltd. First Edition 10th impression 2007}, p 320

Sometimes we maybe commanded by relatives, close friends or maybe employers to do something that is really awful to another human being. We should do as Elifaz did. We should consult with a truly wise and righteous individual.

The Power of Poverty
Yaakov's counsel to Elifaz was to take everything that he had with him because a poor man is considered dead. At the time that Yaakov made this statement to Elifaz regarding poverty, it had to be recognized... it had to be understood by the community in general, by Eisov and by Elifaz that a

poor man is considered the same as a dead man. Now we understand that according to Ha Torah, taking Yaakov's things was not what Eisov meant when he gave the order to kill his brother Yaakov, yet within the broader spectrum of the meaning of being dead Elifaz fulfilled his father's order. The comparison of poverty to death expresses the power poverty has over one! God help us all, please! See Rabbi Yisrael Isser Zvi Herczeg, The Sapirstein Edition Rashi Bereisheit / Genesis {Brooklyn, New York: Mesorah Publications, Ltd. First Edition 10th impression 2007}, p 320

With My Staff
Elifaz heeded his Uncle Yaakov's counsel and took everything but Yaakov's clothes and staff. Undoubtedly the staff appeared to have no value in the eyes of Elifaz or he would have taken it along with the other items. Yet the staff was the most valuable of all Yaakov's possessions. How do we know this? We learn this when Yaakov returns to Eretz Canaan. Our sages say that the correct interpretation of במקלי Vih Mahk Lee "with the use of my staff I crossed the Jordan River." In other words, Yaakov placed his staff into the Yarden River and the Yarden split for him to cross.

With My staff

Mysterious Signs Of The Torah Revealed In GENESIS

במקלי

182 = 10י 30ל 100ק 40מ 2ב

יעקב Yaakov

182 = 2ב 100ק 70ע 10י

The 182 represents the time between Avraham and Yaakov.

It was with this staff that Yaakov first left Eretz Canaan, and then 20 years later returned to Eretz Canaan. It is interesting that the word Haw Yee Tee meaning became has three Yuds. The Letter Yud represents power, i.e. double the strength. We say the Yud is a power letter because the Gematria of the word Yud is exactly double the Gematria of the letter Yud. The word YUD is twenty and the letter Yud is ten.

Ten represents the ten commands of Creation in Bereisheit. Ten represents the Ten Commandments. Ten represents the days of repentance between Rosh Ha Shanah and Yom Kippur. Ten represents the ten righteous that would have spared Sodom and Gomorrah had they existed.

Mysterious Signs Of The Torah Revealed In GENESIS

From the realm of metaphysics we see the power that is represented by ten. Mysticism is metaphysical. There is no basis in reality where Ten Words spoken by HaShem God can be proven to create everything in the universe. One could argue that the Ten Commands exist in a thought, which they do but do not have physical or concrete basis. So what I am sharing is mystical. When the letter Yud {10} is added to a word that normally would not have the letter Yud one should take notice. Power is added. Emphasis is added. Mysticism is added. An example is Bereisheit 2.2 – 4

Bereisheit 2.2 - 4

וַיְכֻלּוּ הַשָּׁמַיִם וְהָאָרֶץ וְכָל־צְבָאָם :

וַיְכַל אֱלֹהִים בַּיּוֹם הַשְּׁבִיעִי מְלַאכְתּוֹ אֲשֶׁר עָשָׂה **וַיִּשְׁבֹּת** בַּיּוֹם הַשְּׁבִיעִי מִכָּל־מְלַאכְתּוֹ אֲשֶׁר עָשָׂה :

וַיְבָרֶךְ אֱלֹהִים אֶת־יוֹם הַשְּׁבִיעִי וַיְקַדֵּשׁ אֹתוֹ כִּי בוֹ **שָׁבַת** מִכָּל־מְלַאכְתּוֹ אֲשֶׁר־בָּרָא אֱלֹהִים לַעֲשׂוֹת :

And He, God Completed the Heavens and the Earth and every host. And He, God Completed by the day, the seventh [day] the work which

Mysterious Signs Of The Torah Revealed In GENESIS

He Made. And He Rested in the Seventh Day from all work that was made. And He, God Blessed everything from the Letter Aleph to the Letter Tav of the Seventh Day and he sanctified it for rest from all work that God created to do. Bereisheit 2.2 - 4

Notice the black letters say וישבת Vah Yee Shi Boht {and He rested}. The first letter of the word וישבת Vah Yee Shi Boht {and He rested} is the letter ו Vav meaning and. The second letter from the right of the word וישבת Vah Yee Shi Boht is the letter י Yud meaning He. Now what is extremely interesting is that from this point on in all of Tenach the letter Yud is not again connected to Esau {rest} with one exception. That exception is in Isaiah. That exception is a repeat of what Bereisheit 2:2 is saying, which is that *'and He rested in day seven.'* What is the point to this? Because the letter Yud represents power, it was included to emphasize rest from creating.

Notice the second set of black letters say שבת Esau {rest}. Our Creator, Blessed is His Name, removed the Yud after Bereisheit 2.2. While the Yud represents *'He'* it also represents work. As in the Ten Commands... The Yud represents added strength. This is especially noted in that God, the Creator is *'All Powerful.'* When the Yud representing our Blessed Creator was removed that in essence removed power from Vah Yee Shi Boht making it Shaw Baht - *'Esau'* as it appears in Bereisheit 2.3.

Now we return to the point regarding three Yuds in the word הייתי Haw Yee Tee which means Yaakov became... Yaakov turned into two camps. The three Yuds represent the strength of this change. Each Yud in the full sense represents twenty instead of ten. Again, Yaakov served his father in law for twenty years.

Yud י = the number ten. The Gematria Miluy for the Letter Yud is equals 20 = יוד when spelled out. So, in twenty years Yaakov became strong and became two camps.

We have another interesting span of time that covers the period of the covenant.

We see this in the mysticism of six names:
Spiritualist / Noachide Covenant The Gematria totals of Shem and Eiver represent the Spiritualist the

Mysterious Signs Of The Torah Revealed In GENESIS

Noachide covenant with our Creator = 612: Shem = 340 years and Eiver = 272 years.

Shem

340 = 40 מ 300 ש

Eiver

272 = 200 ר 2 ב 70 ע

The connection of Shem and Eiver is through the Gematria of their names. Shem lived in the old world before the flood. Shem and Eiver were the righteous descendants of Noach, with whom HaShem made the covenant of the rainbow representing that He would never destroy the entire world by rain again. Shem was a witness to this covenant. The tents of Shem and Eiver are recognized as the school of Shem and Eiver where Ha Torah was taught. Shem and Eiver taught the Spiritualist law and tradition given to Adam and Noach. In Bereisheit 14.18 *Malki Tzedek {Shem}, the King of Shalem, brought out bread and wine...* to Avraham. Rashi comments that *Midrash Aggadah [explains] that he [Malki Tzedek] intimated to him {Avraham} regarding the meal offerings {by giving him bread} and the libations {by giving him wine} that his [Avraham's] descendants would offer there {in Yerushalayim}.* Each of these are alluded to by the fact that Ha Torah states, *He was a Kohein of the Most High Almighty.* The Midrash states that originally *HaShem desired to make Shem the forefather of all Kohanim, but since he [Shem] blessed Avram before blessing his Creator, HaShem took the kehuna away from Shem and gave it to Avram instead.* This is the path where righteous parental influence leads...

The Jewish Covenant The total years of the lives of Avraham, Yitzchok, Yaakov and Yoseif represent the Jewish covenant with our Creator = 612:

Avraham	175 years	Bereisheit 25.7
Yitzchok	180 years	Bereisheit 35.28
Yaakov	147 years	Bereisheit 47.28
Yoseif	110 years	Bereisheit 50.26
Total Years	612 years	

It was to Avraham that Yitzchok was born. Understanding the separation between Avram and

Mysterious Signs Of The Torah Revealed In GENESIS

Avraham is important. The name change of Avram and Sarai to Avraham and Sarah represents the transition from Spirituality to Judaism. Avram and Sarai were Spiritualists. Avraham and Sarah were Jews. When Avram became Avraham and when Sarai became Sarah the promised covenant began. The covenant of Judaism with our Creator began one year before the birth of Yitzchok. The covenant of Judaism began months before the conception of Yitzchok. Classmates, what is the point? Their names were changed well in advance of the conception. Ishmael was born to Avram when he was a Spiritualist. Ishmael was the son of Avram. Ishmael was not the son of Avraham. The Gematria of Avram and Ishmael or Avraham and Ishmael do not add up to bris {covenant / 612}. See Bereisheit 17.9,18 - 21. Our Creator Made it clear in Ha Torah that His covenant was with Avraham and the descendants after him. In other words, the covenant was ONLY to the descendants of Avraham and Sarah.

Brit / Covenant

612 = 400 ת 10 י 200 ר 2 ב

Mysterious Signs Of The Torah Revealed In GENESIS

Realizing Our Creator in Every Action
Chapter 9

Bereisheit Vayeishev
Bereisheit / Genesis 37.1 - 40.23

Bereisheit 39.2

וַיְהִי יְהוָה אֶת־יוֹסֵף וַיְהִי אִישׁ מַצְלִיחַ
וַיְהִי בְּבֵית אֲדֹנָיו הַמִּצְרִי:

And the L-rd existed in everything from the first letter of the Aleph Bet to the last Letter of the Aleph Bet with Yoseif and he managed to be a successful man and he prevailed in the house of his master there in Mitzriam. Bereisheit 39.2

Mysterious Signs Of The Torah Revealed In GENESIS

God Willing, we are going to discover how Yoseif existed, how he managed, how he prevailed in such a challenging climate.

Yoseif is a great example of realizing God in every action. Yoseif does not forsake HaShem. Yoseif remains true to the covenant with his Creator even though he experiences very difficult trials.

There are times in our lives where we may feel entirely abandoned by those we love and those who we are related to. I cannot describe the pain, the agony, the torture, the extreme discomfort of coming to grips with how awful it feels to learn that the very special person in your life no longer loves you. I learned this painful lesson. Trying to describe what it feels like is not necessary. I felt like being in that horrible place was more than a human soul could bear. I have never experienced such utter humiliating, numbing cold hearted rejection as this. Had I not experienced this, it would not be possible for me to know what it is like to be deceived and hated to this deep, deep extent. For a while it felt like there was nothing left in life. Life still had meaning but it felt like everything in life that was important was ripped away. I felt like a weed that had been yanked out of the soil in the most vicious fashion and discarded.

Yoseif experienced these emotions. Yoseif was a great man! He is a champion for those who have been betrayed, for those who have been rejected by those they deeply love, for those who have deceived and lied, and for those who are innocent, but found guilty. I have not come close to his place of loss, humiliation, pain, suffering or numbness, yet where I am, it feels pretty awful.

It is very important for each human being to connect with Yoseif. It is real important to identify with Yoseif. God Willing, this will help us to be careful with how we treat others. God Willing if we can mentally climb inside of the space Yoseif was in, we will be much more understanding.

Pharaoh said to Yoseif, *'See, I have set you in charge over all the land of Mitzriam.'* Bereisheit 41.41 This is a bold statement by Pharaoh. Yet, that is what one would expect from Pharaoh. Ha Torah States, *And HaShem was with Yoseif.* Mystically we can see how HaShem was with Yoseif. The Gematria of the word ויהי Vah Yih Hee is 31. This is the same Gematria of אל El, God Strength.

Mysterious Signs Of The Torah Revealed In GENESIS

Yoseif Existed, Managed and Prevailed...

31 = 10 י 5 ה 10 י 6 ו

God in the Attribute of Strength

31 = 30 ל 1 א

We learn how our Creator was with Yoseif.

וַיְהִי יְהוָה אֶת־יוֹסֵף

And the L-rd existed in everything from the first letter of the Aleph Bet to the last Letter of the Aleph Bet with Yoseif...

First, God's Strength was with Yoseif everywhere in everything!

וַיְהִי אִישׁ מַצְלִיחַ

...and he managed to be a successful man ...

Second, in actuality, God's Strength made Yoseif a successful man.

Mysterious Signs Of The Torah Revealed In GENESIS

וַיְהִי בְּבֵית אֲדֹנָיו הַמִּצְרִי:

and he prevailed in the house of his master there in Mitzriam.

Third, God's Strength was with Yoseif in the master's house.

The word ויהי Vah Yih Hee is used three times in the same Passuk. 3 times 31 = 93.

Bereisheit 15.1

אַחַר ׀ הַדְּבָרִים הָאֵלֶּה הָיָה דְבַר־יְהֹוָה אֶל־אַבְרָם בַּמַּחֲזֶה לֵאמֹר אַל־תִּירָא אַבְרָם אָנֹכִי **מָגֵן** לָךְ שְׂכָרְךָ הַרְבֵּה מְאֹד:

After these things, HaShem's Word Existed to Avram in a vision vocalizing, 'Do not fear Avram, I am your shield, and your reward is very great, **Bereisheit 15.1.**

The word that we should be immediately observing is מגן Maw Gayn, meaning shield. The three different instances we observe Yoseif facing, add up

Mysterious Signs Of The Torah Revealed In GENESIS

to HaShem being a shield for him.

Yoseif Existed, Managed and Prevailed... - Vah Yeh Hee

93 = 3 x 31 = 10 י 5 ה 10 י 6 ו

Shield - Maw Gayn

93 = 50 ן 3 ג 40 מ

Notice the Gematria of Vah Yih Hee - HaShem - Ehs Yoseif, {And HaShem was with Yoseif} is 614. This is like saying there are 613 mitzvahs plus Pharaoh, when in fact it is Mystically stating how HaShem was with Yoseif. HaShem was with Yoseif in his complete Torah observance. So we have Yoseif's total observance of Torah plus the result {One}, God was with him. In other words, complete Torah observance results in God's presence being with us.

614 = 80 ף 60 ס 6 ו 10 י   400 ת 1 א   5 ה 6 ו 5 ה 10 י   10 י 5 ה 10 י 6 ו

614 = 400 ת 10 י 200 ר 2 ב 2 ב

This is an excellent example of how we can observe HaShem with us. This story of Yoseif is a Mystical example of HaShem's presence with us in Strength and as a Shield all the time. Thank God!

We need to exert our being to realize HaShem in every action as represented by Gematria 614, where Ha Torah stated, "And HaShem was with Yoseif." This represents the blessings of the observant life. HaShem is with us in everything. We need to avoid situations where others fail to acknowledge God in every action. Pharaoh's failure to acknowledge God in every action was represented by the Gematria 612.

So on the one hand we have an issue with Pharaoh, who desires to take all the credit for placing Yoseif atop his house and his kingdom. We see this mystically in the Gematria 612. He desires to make the covenant, the agreement, with Yoseif as opposed to the True Power behind Yoseif, The God of all Creation. Pharaoh attempts to skirt around the true King, the King of all Kings, the King over All Kings! He unrightfully attempts to take credit for Yoseif's surge to power.

When Pharaoh desired to make Yoseif the second in command over all Mitzriam / Egypt Pharaoh's astrologers exclaimed: *Will you place in power over us a slave whom his master purchased for twenty pieces of silver!*
Pharaoh replied to them, *I discern in him royal*

characteristics.

They said to him, *In that case he must be acquainted with the seventy languages.*

[The Angel] Gabriel came [that night] and taught [Joseph] the seventy languages, but he could not learn them. Thereupon [Gabriel] added to his name a letter from the Name of the Holy One, blessed be [Gabriel], and [Yoseif] learned [the 70 languages] as it is said:

'He appointed it in Joseph for a testimony, when he went out over the land of Egypt, where I [Joseph] heard a language that I knew not.'
[Tehillim / Psalms 81.6 and Sota 10b, 36b] When the wife of Potiphar attempted to seduce יוסף, Joseph, in the privacy of her home, Joseph feared [God} and refused to give in to temptation. Because he sanctified [God's] Name, he merited that the letter ה, Hey from [God's] Name should be added to his own, making it יהוסף, (Sotah 10b). The Talmud (Sotah 36b) offers yet another reason why he letter ה, Hey was inserted in Joseph's name: Pharaoh was deeply impressed by Joseph's wisdom when Joseph interpreted his dream, and he wished to elevate Joseph to the post of viceroy. However, Pharaoh's counselors reminded him that an Egyptian statute stipulated that pointees to royal positions must know the seventy languages of the world. That night, the angel Gabriel attempted to teach Joseph all seventy languages. The angel's efforts were unsuccessful until he added the letter ה, Hey from [God's] Name to Joseph's Name. As a result, Joseph became inspired and grasped the spiritual content of each language. Soon he knew all seventy tongues and was fit for the royal post. Rabbi Avrohom Chaim Feuer and Rabbi Nosson Scherman The Artscroll Tanach Series - Tehillim Volume 2 -

Mysterious Signs Of The Torah Revealed In GENESIS

(Brooklyn New York: Mesorah Publications, Ltd. 3rd Impression 1991), pp 1028, 1029

On the morrow, [Rosh HaShanah] in whatever language Pharaoh conversed with [Joseph] he replied to him; but when [Joseph] spoke to [Pharaoh] in the holy tongue [Pharaoh] did not understand what he said. So [Pharaoh] asked [Joseph] to teach it to him; [Joseph] taught it to him but he could not learn it. [Pharaoh] said to him, *'Swear to me that thou wilt not reveal this'* (i.e. that Pharaoh was ignorant of Hebrew, and a king was expected to know every language.) and [Joseph swore to him.

[Joseph] later said to [Pharaoh], *My father made me swear, saying, 'Behold I am dying. In my grave that I have prepared for myself in the land of Canaan, Listen!, there shall you bury me,* Bereisheit 50.5,6.

[Pharaoh] remarked to him, *Go, ask [to be released from] your oath.*

[Joseph] replied to him, *'I will also ask [to be released from my oath] concerning you'*

Therefore, although it was displeasing to him,

Mysterious Signs Of The Torah Revealed In GENESIS

[Pharaoh] said to him, *Go up and bury your father, according as he made you swear,* Bereisheit 50.7. See Sota 36b

The point is that Pharaoh made i.e. extracted from Yoseif a covenant, an agreement, a pledge a promise that Yoseif would not reveal that Pharaoh did not know all seventy languages as required for a king.

Pharaoh took credit for knowing all seventy languages. Our Creator, Pharaoh and Yoseif knew the truth. A a result he required that Yoseif swear that he would not reveal this secret. Dear ones, we must be very careful to realize God's presence in every action! Beneath the mirky waters is the possibility for dry land. Yet we only realize what God already knows when He speaks the words ותראה היבשה Vih Tay Raw Eh - Hah Yah Baw Shawh {and let [it, the dry land] appear}. So while Pharaoh thought it was his words that confirmed Yoseif as Viceroy of Mitzriam, it actually was HaShem from the Heavens saying 'And let appear Yoseif'. The Gematria for ותראה Vih Say Raw Eh is 612.

Vih Say Raw Eh {and let [Yoseif] appear}

612 = 5ה 1א 200ר 400ת 6ו

Brit / Covenant

Mysterious Signs Of The Torah Revealed In GENESIS

612 = 400ת 10י 200ר 2ב

We need to exert our being to realize HaShem in every action as represented by Gematrias within the Words of Ha Torah *And HaShem was with Yoseif*. This represents the blessings of our Creator in very action on the observant life.

Mysterious Signs Of The Torah Revealed In GENESIS

Mysterious Signs Of The Torah Revealed In GENESIS

Osnat, A Praiseworthy Wife
Chapter 10

Bereisheit Mikeitz
Bereisheit / Genesis 41.1 - 44.17

Bereisheit 41.45

וַיִּקְרָא פַרְעֹה שֵׁם־יוֹסֵף צָפְנַת פַּעְנֵחַ וַיִּתֶּן־
לוֹ **אֶת־אָסְנַת** בַּת־פּוֹטִי פֶרַע כֹּהֵן אֹן לְאִשָּׁה
וַיֵּצֵא יוֹסֵף עַל־אֶרֶץ מִצְרָיִם׃

And he, Pharaoh proclaimed Yoseif's [Egyptian] name Tzaw Pih Nat - Paheh Nay Ach and he gave everything from Aleph to Tav of Awsnat daughter of Poti Phera, Priest of On, for a wife, and He, Yoseif, emerged over the land of Mitzriam.   Bereisheit 41.45

Mysterious Signs Of The Torah Revealed In GENESIS

In Parshat Mikeitz an interesting name surfaces. The name is אסנת Osnat, wife of Yoseif. When we think of אסנת Osnat we should immediately think of אשרי Ahsh Ray... We should think of her as an individual who is praiseworthy. We should also think of תקוה Teek Vaw... We should think of Osnat as a woman of hope and expectation.

As a child Osnat was driven from Yaakov's house by her uncles according to Pirkei d'Rabbi Eliezer. This was because her uncles were concerned that people would speak of licentiousness in their tents. They were concerned that people would think that they were morally perverse. As a result Yaakov engraved a metal plate and put it around Osnat' neck to protect her. The metal plate was engraved with words to the effect that Osnat' parents were Shechem and Deenah and that whoever married her would be marrying a relative of Yaakov's family.

At this point Osnat was placed under a bush in a field and left. Her name is a derivative of the word Si Neh {thorn bush}. Through providence a Malach {messenger} took Osnat from under the thorn bush to the house of Potiphar in Mitzriam. He and his wife raised her as their own daughter. Twenty-two years later Pharaoh ordered that Osnat marry Yoseif to vindicate Yoseif from any guilt brought on by the false accusation of her foster mother, Potiphar's wife. Potiphar's wife accused Yoseif of sexual assault. It is at this point that we make mention of the fact that the Midrash points out, that at every birth of Yaakov's sons a twin daughter was born. The purpose was so that the sons could marry sisters as wives. However when Yoseif was born without a twin sister this was a sign that Yoseif would marry someone else, Osnat. See Rabbi Meir Zlotowitz and Rabbi Nosson Scherman, The Artscroll Tanach Series - Bereishis Vol. I(b) (Brooklyn, New York: Mesorah Publications, Ltd. 3rd Impression, 1989), pp 1800, 1801; Rabbi Dr. H. Freedman, Midrash Rabba (New York, NY: The Soncino Press 1983) - Midrash Rabbah writes, *Tamar was the daughter of Shem.* p 829

Dear ones, just as Yoseif ascended to viceroy of Mitzriam from a lowly position of prisoner, Osnat ascended to be his wife from the lowly position of a deserted baby under a thorn bush. By providence they were brought together.

For 22 years Osnat was raised in aristocratic culture. She was the adopted daughter of a pagan priest, yet Ha Torah states *'to Yoseif were born two sons before the famine years set in from Osnat daughter of Potiphar...'* This brief seemingly unimportant statement is extremely important. It is important because here Torah identifies Menasheh and Ephraim as "Yoseif's sons." They were not the grandsons of an idolatrous priest of Mitzriam. Yet they could have been, God forbid! It was the mother's choice. Osnat chose to reconnect with Judaism prior to her marriage to Yoseif. Why do you suppose she chose to do this? It was because she was not idolatrous! She was Jewish! She was the daughter of a Jew! Even though she had been raised as a pagan for 22 years, the flame of Torah Judaism did not go out in her Neshamah!

From the inscription on the plate around her neck left under a bush she knew that she was a descendant of Yaakov as was Yoseif. Somehow this surfaced. Maybe it was when Osnat' foster mother said these words to her husband, " He brought us this Hebrew to mock us..." Our sages say that the "us" in Potiphar's wife's accusation was directed at the other women in the house... the slave women in the house. Yet the impact was felt by another woman... a Hebrew... an adopted daughter who knew her foster mother's passions and lies... This was Osnat. And like a thorn bush she bristled at what was said. At this point she was approaching the age of Bat Mitzvah.

Mysterious Signs Of The Torah Revealed In GENESIS

Remember Yoseif was six years old when Yaakov left Padan Aram. Yaakov settled in Shechem for two years. He was away from his father for 22 years according to our sages, 20 years in Padan Aram and two years in the city of Shechem. His reason for leaving at the end of two years was the retribution Shimon and Levi took against Shechem for the kidnapping and defilement of their sister Deenah. At this time Yoseif would have been eight years old. Nine years later he was sold into slavery {at the age of seventeen}. He served in Potiphar's house for over one year. At this time Osnat was about the age of nine.

Osnat being a member of the house could have heard her foster mother Zulaicha falsely accuse Yoseif. She could have heard the conspiracy that Zulaicha schemed, instructing the other women in the house to follow against Yoseif... We don't know. Yet we do notice that Ha Torah states, "Osnat was the daughter of Potiphar" So from this brief statement we learn much.

Here the implication seems to be a rejection of her foster mother and what she attempted to do to Yoseif. Ha Torah notes this division. According to our sages providence brought Osnat to Potiphar not to Zulaicha. In addition it is possible that this Torah distinction was made because Potiphar may have had several wives. Nonetheless, Osnat is not identified with Zulaicha. This combined with her return to Judaism points to a righteousness not openly discussed.

We know that Yoseif would not have married outside of his household. So we know at some point this connection had to be revealed to both of them. Mystically the greatness is noted in Osnat. The Gematria of her name is 511. This is the same Gematria as that of Ahsh Ray {praiseworthy} and Teek Vaw {expectation}. Osnat is praiseworthy for rejecting the lies of Zulaicha. Osnat is praiseworthy for returning to Judaism and she is praiseworthy for raising her children by Yoseif's tradition instead of her own. Her praiseworthiness is so great that all Judaism blesses their children as Yaakov blessed Ephraim and Menasheh.

Aws Nays / Aws Nayt {daughter of Deenah}

511 = 400ת 50נ 60ס 1א

Mysterious Signs Of The Torah Revealed In GENESIS

Ahsh Ray {Praiseworthy}

511 = 10 י 200 ר 300 ש 1 א

Teek Vaw {Hope Expectation}

511 = 5 ה 6 ו 100 ק 400 ת

In addition to this we observe an expectation Mystically hidden in her name. One must ask what was that expectation? I believe that expectation was to meet the man who inscribed the words... "This child Osnat' parents were Shechem and Deenah and whoever marries her is marrying a relative of Yaakov's family.'

Within the names of יוסף Yoseif and אסנת Osnat is a most unusual letter, the Letter Samech. This is quite unusual because the letter Samech is rare in Ha Torah. The letter Samech represents support, protection and memory. Rabbi Michael Munk The Wisdom In The Hebrew Alphabet Mesorah Publications, Brooklyn, N.Y. 1990), p. 159

The following words begin with the letter Samech. ספר = book, סדר = order / set; סוף = End and סימן = sign.

Mysterious Signs Of The Torah Revealed In GENESIS

אֶת־אָסְנַת

Aws Nays / Aws Nayt {daughter of Deenah}

511 = 400ת 50נ 60ס 1א

- LESS {minus}

Eht {Everything from the Letter א Aleph to the Letter ת Tav}

401 = 400ת 1א

110 = 511 − 401
What is significant of the number 110?   Yoseif lived 110 years, Bereisheit 50.26

Mysterious Signs Of The Torah Revealed In GENESIS

Gematria Footprints of Yoseif
Chapter 11

Bereisheit Vayigash
Bereisheit / Genesis 44.18 - 47.27

Bereisheit 45.19

וְאַתָּה **צֻוֵּיתָה** זֹאת עֲשׂוּ קְחוּ־לָכֶם מֵאֶרֶץ מִצְרַיִם עֲגָלוֹת לְטַפְּכֶם וְלִנְשֵׁיכֶם וּנְשָׂאתֶם אֶת־אֲבִיכֶם וּבָאתֶם :

And you are commanded [to have your brothers do] this work. [Each of] you, take wagons from the land of Mitzriam to your children and to your wives everything from the letter Aleph to the letter Tav to your father and bring them [to Mitzriam]. Bereisheit 45.19

Mysterious Signs Of The Torah Revealed In GENESIS

In Parshat Mikeitz we discussed the Gematria 511 and the relationships to Osnat, Yoseif's wife, and her praiseworthiness and her hope of meeting her grandfather Yaakov, who placed a special inscription around her neck that saved her life. That hope, that praise is realized in this week's parshat. And in addition to this, we realize other important Gematrias. Ha Torah states that when Pharaoh heard of Yoseif's brothers and father, he צִוִּיתָה *Tzu Vay Taw {commanded}...* Pharaoh commanded that they take wagons from Mitzriam to transport Yoseif's relatives to Canaan and back to Mitzriam. He commanded that Yoseif's relatives should not be concerned with their belongings. He commanded that the best of Mitzriam be provided for Yoseif's relatives.

Tzu Vay Taw {Commanded}

511 = 5ה 400ת 10י 6ו 90צ

Holy reader, we observe Pharaoh reacting to his appreciation for Yoseif. We observe Pharaoh reacting to the painful separation between Yoseif and his family. We observe Pharaoh sharing in Yoseif's joy and in Osnat's joy.

Mysterious Signs Of The Torah Revealed In GENESIS

One must ask when did all this begin? It began with a dream and ended with a dream. It began with Yoseif's dream in Bereishis 37.7. This is where Yoseif told his father and his brothers that their sheaves prostrated themselves לַאֲלֻמָּתִי *Lah Ah Lu Maw Tee {to my sheaf}*. Yoseif's dream and his interpretation of his dream angered his father and his brothers. Let's say it gave Yoseif's brothers a strong shove to sell Yoseif into slavery. The Gematria of Lah Ah Lu Maw Tee {to my sheaf} is also 511.

Bereisheit 37.7

וְהִנֵּה אֲנַחְנוּ מְאַלְּמִים אֲלֻמִּים בְּתוֹךְ הַשָּׂדֶה וְהִנֵּה קָמָה אֲלֻמָּתִי וְגַם־נִצָּבָה וְהִנֵּה תְסֻבֶּינָה אֲלֻמֹּתֵיכֶם וַתִּשְׁתַּחֲוֶיןָ לַאֲלֻמָּתִי׃

And behold, we were building sheaves in the midst of the field. And behold, my sheaf ascended and even stood straight, and behold, your sheaves surrounded [my sheaf] and prostrated themselves **to my sheaf.** **Bereisheit 37.7**

Mysterious Signs Of The Torah Revealed In GENESIS

Lah Ah Lu Maw Tee {To my sheaf}

511 = 10 י‎ 400 ת‎ 40 מ‎ 30 ל‎ 1 א‎ 30 ל‎

Next we revisit, we return to a Hebrew slave who was kidnapped, sold into slavery, falsely accused and imprisoned. That individual was Yoseif. Then he was twenty-eight years old. This was eleven years after being sold into slavery. He is now listening to the dreams of Pharaoh's Chief Butler and Chief Baker. In the dream of the Chief Baker we read the word ראשׁי‎ Roh Shee {my head} which also has the Gematria of 511. It is here that we observe that the Chief Baker's head was removed. Dear ones, this is not by chance, this is Torah Mysticism!! This is the Mystical connection woven through the pages of Ha Torah of HaShem. It was this incident that remained deeply imbedded in the memory of the Chief Butler who later spoke of this Hebrew slave in the dungeon to Pharaoh.

Bereisheit 40.16

וַיַּרְא שַׂר־הָאֹפִים כִּי טוֹב פָּתָר וַיֹּאמֶר
אֶל־יוֹסֵף אַף־אֲנִי בַּחֲלוֹמִי וְהִנֵּה
שְׁלֹשָׁה סַלֵּי חֹרִי עַל־רֹאשִׁי׃

Mysterious Signs Of The Torah Revealed In GENESIS

Bereisheit 40.16, 17

וּבַסַּל הָעֶלְיוֹן מִכֹּל מַאֲכַל פַּרְעֹה מַעֲשֵׂה אֹפֶה וְהָעוֹף אֹכֵל אֹתָם מִן־הַסַּל מֵעַל רֹאשִׁי׃

And he, the Chief Baker saw, for the interpretation was good. And he said to Yoseif, I also dreamed. And behold were three baskets on my head. **Bereisheit 40.16**

And in the higher basket were all food dishes for Pharaoh, prepared baked [pastries] and the birds were eating them from my basket from upon my head, **Bereisheit 40.17.**

Roh Shee {My head}

511 = 10 י 300 ש 1 א 200 ר

After Pharaoh gives the command that we began with, we observe the result of that command. Ha Torah states that *the sons of Yisroel transported everything from Aleph to Tav of their father Yaakov and everything from Aleph to Tav of their children and everything from Aleph to Tav of their wives* בָּעֲגָלוֹת *Baw Ah Gaw Loht {in wagons}*. Bereisheit 46.6 Baw Ah Gaw Loht has the Gematria 511.

Mysterious Signs Of The Torah Revealed In GENESIS

Bereisheit 46.6

וַיָּקָם יַעֲקֹב מִבְּאֵר שָׁבַע וַיִּשְׂאוּ בְנֵי־יִשְׂרָאֵל אֶת־יַעֲקֹב אֲבִיהֶם וְאֶת־טַפָּם וְאֶת־נְשֵׁיהֶם **בָּעֲגָלוֹת** אֲשֶׁר־שָׁלַח פַּרְעֹה לָשֵׂאת אֹתוֹ׃

*And Arose, Yaakov from Beer Sheva, and the sons of Yisroel transported everything from Aleph to Tav of him, Yaakov their father, and everything from Aleph to Tav of the children, and everything from Aleph to Tav of their wives **in wagons** that Pharaoh sent to carry them [to Mitzriam].*

Baw Ah Gaw Loht {in wagons}

511 = 400ת 6ו 30ל 3ג 70ע 2ב

511 = Tav 400 Vav 6 Lamid 30 Gimmel 3 Ayin 70 Bet 2

In the last chapter we observed this holy connection in relation to Osnat. In this chapter we observe this holy connection surrounding Yoseif and his dreams. In both instances we mystically observe the Gematria footprints of Yoseif and Osnat and Divine providence guiding... directing at difficult places in their lives through the Gematria of 511.

For nine years Pharaoh, the ruler of Mitzriam, knew Yoseif in a microscopic way. He understood that Yoseif was a sage. Ha Torah Records Pharaoh as saying,
Bereishis 41.39

וַיֹּאמֶר פַּרְעֹה אֶל־יוֹסֵף אַחֲרֵי הוֹדִיעַ
אֱלֹהִים אוֹתְךָ אֶת־כָּל־זֹאת אֵין־נָבוֹן
וְחָכָם כָּמוֹךָ:

The unwritten intention of what Pharaoh said is as follows:
And said Pharaoh to Yoseif, [you, who were] behind [being sold into slavery, falsely accused, imprisoned, etc.] [you were the one] notified by the attribute of God's Justice. You have the sign from Aleph to Tav of all this. No one is as clever and as wise like you are.

Now prior to this, following Pharaoh's dream, he had summoned the best wise men of Mitzriam to explain his dream. None could. It was then that the Chief Butler stepped forward and spoke to Pharaoh regarding Yoseif. He described Yoseif as *a lad, a Hebrew, a slave to the Chief Executioner...*

Bereishis 41.12. Ha Torah What an introduction to the King of Mitzriam. Then Ha Torah goes on to describe Yoseif's physical condition. Yoseif was in a dungeon. He needed a haircut and a shave. He needed a bath and clean clothes. In other words, his physical condition was not presentable to Pharaoh.

Knowing all this about Yoseif after Yoseif explained Pharaoh's dream, Pharaoh responded,   *...[you, who were] behind [being sold into slavery, falsely accused and imprisoned, etc.] [were the one] notified by the attribute of God's Justice. You have the sign from Aleph to Tav of all this. No one is as clever and as wise like you are,* Bereishis 41.39.

It was clear to Pharaoh that Yoseif had the sign from God. God, Pharaoh and Yoseif made a connection. Pharaoh understood that God selected this Hebrew slave in the prison dungeon of his Chief Executioner to be the man with the message. One must wonder, how did this feel to the King of Mitzriam? One must wonder, what was the underlying message of the message? How could God have chosen this man of the lowliest means and situation to deliver such an important message?

Pharaoh called for the Hebrew prisoner slave... He listened. He made an immediate analysis of what Yoseif said. He acknowledged Yoseif's wisdom in the presence of his kingly cabinet. He immediately promoted Yoseif because he understood that God had selected Yoseif. Pharaoh understood God had given Yoseif the sign.

Before Yoseif even heard Pharaoh's dream he said to Pharaoh, *God will respond from Aleph to Tav in Peace regarding Pharaoh's dream.* The KJV says, *God will give Pharaoh an answer of peace,* Bereisheit 41.16. Dear ones, what is the point to this? Holy classmate, Yoseif was establishing a fact with Pharaoh. God gave Pharaoh the dream and God would answer Pharaoh's dream in a satisfactory way after he, Yoseif, explained the details to Pharaoh.

We are observing the microscopic connection between God, Pharaoh and Yoseif. Pharaoh was an insightful king. He was wise. He was not afraid to make a decision. He acknowledged that Yoseif, this Hebrew slave who just an hour ago was in the prison dungeon of his Chief Executioner, was the man with God's message. Pharaoh said to his servants, to his kingly cabinet, that Yoseif was the man. Pharaoh said, *'the Spirit of God dwells in him.* Then

Pharaoh continued on, *Yoseif, [you, who were] behind [being sold into slavery, falsely accused, imprisoned, etc.] [were the one] notified by the attribute of God's justice. You have the sign from Aleph to Tav of all this. No one is as clever and as wise like you are'*, Bereisheit 41.39. Then Pharaoh promoted Yoseif. Then Pharaoh gave Yoseif his signet ring as a sign of his promotion. Then Pharaoh dressed Yoseif in King's clothing and gave him a gold chain to wear around his neck. He ordered that Yoseif would immediately follow him in processional as the second chariot and that the people of Mitzriam would call out 'king' as Yoseif passed. Pharaoh gave Yoseif a name. Pharaoh selected a Jewish wife for Yoseif. Pharaoh straightened out the misunderstanding that sent Yoseif to prison. Yet there was one thing Pharaoh could not straighten out. With all his power and influence there was one thing he could not do. That would have to wait. It was this thing that brings us to this week's parshat.

Pharaoh could not share the joy of a family with Yoseif. Even though he had the power to search for Yoseif's family he couldn't. Why couldn't he? Yoseif had the sign from God! Pharaoh clearly understood the power of this sign. This is evidenced by all that

Pharaoh did for Yoseif. And it is evidenced by what Pharaoh did not do! Pharaoh did not send messengers to Canaan in search of Yoseif's family. Pharaoh did not interfere in any way with the power of Yoseif's sign. He knew that Yoseif was kidnapped from his homeland and had the power himself to alter his situation, yet he did not press Yoseif. Pharaoh did not interfere. Pharaoh knew of Yoseif's difficulties yet he could do nothing.

That is, until the day he heard of Yoseif's brothers. From the background Pharaoh observed Yoseif's behavior with these men from Canaan. Knowing that Yoseif was a just and righteous man in whom God's Spirit dwelt, Pharaoh had to be curious when Yoseif accused these men from the land of Canaan of being spies and had them tossed into the dungeon for three days. Holy readers, do not think for one minute that Pharaoh did not follow this situation as it unwrapped. These strange men were accused of being spies. They could have been a threat to the kingdom. Pharaoh knew Yoseif had Shimon thrown in prison. He knew Yoseif ordered that their money be placed in the neck of their sack after their sacks were filled with grain. Pharaoh read the transcript from Yoseif's inquisition of these men. He read Yoseif's peculiar questions about the father and younger brother. Yet Pharaoh did not get involved.

That is until the day he heard of Yoseif's brothers. It was then when Yoseif's family became common knowledge that Pharaoh shared in Yoseif's joy. It was then that Pharaoh gave provisions and wagons to Yoseif's brothers. It was then that we read Pharaoh commanded Yoseif. {Bereishis 45.18} It was then that Pharaoh interfered!

Dear reader, for nine years Pharaoh watched as this unwrapped. He sat back. He observed. Finally the day came when Pharaoh commanded! That was the day that Pharaoh shared in Yoseif's joy.

Learning to Live with Adversity
Chapter 12

Bereisheit Vayechi
Bereisheit / Genesis 47.28 - 50.26

Bereisheit 47.28

וַיְחִי יַעֲקֹב בְּאֶרֶץ מִצְרַיִם שְׁבַע עֶשְׂרֵה שָׁנָה וַיְהִי יְמֵי־יַעֲקֹב שְׁנֵי חַיָּיו שֶׁבַע שָׁנִים וְאַרְבָּעִים וּמְאַת שָׁנָה:

*And he, Yaakov **lived in** [the] land of Mitzriam / Egypt seventeen years. And the days of Yaakov, the years of his life were one hundred forty seven years.* **Bereisheit 47.28**

Mysterious Signs Of The Torah Revealed In GENESIS

Our parshat begins with the words, *'And lived He, Yaakov in the land of Mitzriam for seventeen years...'* Bereisheit 47.28

Did Yaakov want to live outside of Eretz Canaan? No! Is Mitzriam where Yaakov wanted to live? No! Did Yaakov want to die in Mitzriam? No! Dear reader, our sages teach that when Yaakov journeyed to Mitzriam, the remaining five years of the famine immediately ended, upon his entrance into Mitzriam. That being the situation one may wonder / question, 'Then why did Yaakov stay in Mitzriam until his death?' Holy reader, the point is not complex. Even Yaakov the great tzaddik could not just leave Mitzriam and return to Eretz Canaan as he desired. The timing was not right. He had to remain in Mitzriam until his death.

The lesson here is that even though there are Jews who would desire to live in Eretz Yisroel, it may not be possible for them. And even though there are Jews who may strongly desire to live in an observant Jewish Community, it may not be possible for them. There are times that it is necessary to live just where we are. Then there are times that it may be necessary for one to actually move away from the land of Yisroel as Yaakov did. It may be necessary to move away from an observant Jewish community. One may wonder why. It may be for any number of reasons. However our point in this discussion is not to explore the why. Our point is to simply observe the words, *Yaakov lived.* Even though Yaakov preferred to live in Eretz Canaan he lived in Mitzriam. Even though Yaakov preferred to die in Eretz Canaan he lived in Mitzriam, knowing that he would die there.

Holy reader, there is a message in the words "Yaakov lived"! Yaakov was LIVING where he did not want to be. Yaakov was prospering in Mitzriam. Yaakov's children were greatly prospering in Mitzriam. They were not in Eretz Canaan. They were in Mitzriam. This is the point! Yaakov and his descendants lived and prospered in a place other than where they desired to be. This is the message to many of us. Do you think that Yoseif would have rather remained in Mitzriam or returned to Eretz Canaan immediately? It is obvious what Yoseif would have rather done. Yet he remained in Mitzriam. This is a message to those who would rather work somewhere other than where they are. This is a message to those who would rather reside somewhere else. Yaakov lived!

Mysterious Signs Of The Torah Revealed In GENESIS

For many it is not possible to work in the position they desire. For many it is not possible to work in the location they desire. For many it is not possible to live in the country or city they would choose. For many they cannot live in the house they may dream of living in. For many we cannot attend the day school, high school, Bais Yaakov, Yeshiva, prep school, institution, college or university that we truly desire to attend. Yet even when all of these no's exist... when all of these impossibilities exist, understand this: Yaakov lived! We must gravitate to Yaakov's level. We must join Yaakov in living. We must exploit the area of life to the fullest regardless of where we are, where we work or what school we learn in. This is the introduction to Parshat Vayechi. Yaakov Lived!

Even if we lose our position... even if we lose our business or place of employment... even if we lose our family home... even if we lose our children, WE MUST LEARN TO CONTINUE LIVING!

Dear readers, many years ago I lost my position. I lost the family business'. I lost the family home. Then I lost my children and many relatives for awhile. I have been there. I was destitute. I was penniless, I was homeless. I was without transportation. It was not easy! Yet, I needed to learn how Yaakov Lived!

Noach lived during the flood. It was not easy! Avraham was tossed into the fiery furnace. It was not easy! Yitzchok / Isaac offered himself as the willing sacrifice. It was not easy! Yaakov lived with his evil father-in-law for twenty years. It was not easy! God, Please help us all!

When so much does not go the way we desire, we must learn how to live with adversity, affliction, bad luck, calamity, difficulty, distress, hardship, life's misfortunes, misery, pain, sorrow, suffering, trouble, tribulation. We must learn how to live without things we need or desire. Now, I am not saying we cannot have these things. If God Wills, we can have them. Yet, there may be times that we will be required to learn how to live with issues. Again, God please help us all!

When our country is attacked... when peace fails... when our business fails... when we face adversity we must learn how to live! This is what Yaakov taught us! This is what Yoseif taught us. This is what B'nei Yisroel taught us while living as slaves in Mitzriam.

Mysterious Signs Of The Torah Revealed In GENESIS

The absolute importance of us understanding the first two words of Parshat Vayechi, *'Yaakov Lived'* is so important to us living and thriving. Even though Yaakov did not want to reside in the land of Mitzriam, Yaakov Lived! Even though Yaakov did not care to expire in Mitzriam, for seventeen years Yaakov Lived. Yaakov taught us the importance of living in whatever situation we find ourselves. The Gematria of Vayechi Yaakov {Yaakov Lived} is 216.

Vayechi Yaakov {Yaakov Lived}
216 = 2ב 100ק 70ע 10י   10י 8ח 10י 6ו

Now, holy reader, the point to Vayechi Yaakov {Yaakov Lived} is not just the fact that Yaakov lived but HOW Yaakov lived. Mystically we observe that Yaakov had a special peace about himself. Yaakov had a special place of peace within himself that he withdrew to for renewal, and to receive encouragement, strength, guidance and assistance. One could say that Yaakov lived within a protected place. This protective place is revealed to us in Bereisheit 35.7 where Ha Torah says, וַיִּקְרָא לַמָּקוֹם and he called to [the] place אֵל בֵּית־אֵל God is [the] House of God, i.e. There is a Spiritual place which is called the House of God. God dwells there. It is a Spiritual place. It is not a physical house.

Mysterious Signs Of The Torah Revealed In GENESIS

Bereisheit 35.7

וַיִּבֶן שָׁם מִזְבֵּחַ וַיִּקְרָא לַמָּקוֹם אֵל בֵּית־אֵל כִּי שָׁם נִגְלוּ אֵלָיו הָאֱלֹהִים בְּבָרְחוֹ מִפְּנֵי אָחִיו:

And He built [בנה] there [שם] an altar and he called to [the] place, God, House of God, for their God was revealed [נגלה] to him when he fled from his brother.

The point that is necessary to make here is that Yaakov's life frequently faced adversity, affliction, calamity, difficulty, distress, hardship, life's misfortunes, misery, pain, sorrow, suffering, trouble, tribulation... EVEN THOUGH HE WAS A RIGHTEOUS MAN.

Ha Torah records the difficulty Yaakov faced from the moment of conception until his departing. When Yaakov spoke with Pharaoh he said, '...*few and troublesome have been the days of my life...,*' Bereisheit 47.9.

Bereisheit 47.9

וַיֹּאמֶר יַעֲקֹב אֶל־פַּרְעֹה יְמֵי שְׁנֵי מְגוּרַי שְׁלֹשִׁים וּמְאַת שָׁנָה מְעַט וְרָעִים הָיוּ יְמֵי שְׁנֵי חַיַּי וְלֹא הִשִּׂיגוּ אֶת־יְמֵי שְׁנֵי חַיֵּי אֲבֹתַי בִּימֵי מְגוּרֵיהֶם:

Mysterious Signs Of The Torah Revealed In GENESIS

And He, Yaakov said to Pharaoh, 'The days [יְמֵי] of my years [שְׁנֵי] sojourning are one hundred thirty years. Few and difficult have been the days of my life. I have not attained from Aleph to Tav of the years of my father's life in the days of my sojourning.'

Clashes in the womb
The children [Eisov / Esau and Yaakov / Jacob] clashed inside her {Rivkah / Rebecca]... Bereisheit 25.21

Yaakov and Eisov have adversity at the age of fifteen
Yaakov was preparing a pot of red lentils. Why? His Grandfather Avraham had died. Rabbi Meir Zlotowitz and Rabbi Nosson Scherman, The Artscroll Tanach Series - Bereishis Vol. I(b) (Brooklyn, New York: Mesorah Publications, Ltd. 3rd Impression, 1989), p 1066 Eisov wanted to eat the mourners dish of red lentils that Yaakov was preparing for his father. See Bereisheit 25..29-34.

Yaakov is affiliated at the age of forty when Eisov marries idolatrous women.
Ha Torah says, 'They were a source of Spiritual bitterness to Yitzchok and Rivkah, Bereisheit 26.35. What about Yaakov? Were they a source of difficulty

for Yaakov? Yes! Why? They worshiped idols, God Forbid! They offered / burned incense to idols. The pagan worship was obvious because the sounds from their voices and the smell of the incense traveled into the tents [residences] of those around them. See Bereisheit 26.34 - 27.1.

Yaakov faced distress when Yitzchok, their father blessed him.

See Bereisheit 27. Ha Torah records that, Eisov hated Yaakov and intended to kill him. Yaakov fled from his brother.

Yaakov endured calamity with Lavan and his sons

Lavan switched wives on Yaakov, Bereisheit 29.18-30.

Lavan changed his wages many times, Bereisheit 31.41.

Lavan's sons were distressed with Yaakov, Bereisheit 31.1.

Yaakov struggles with super natural beings

Yaakov wrestled with Eisov's guardian angel, Bereisheit 32.26 – 33

Yaakov prepares to face Eisov in battle.

Mysterious Signs Of The Torah Revealed In GENESIS

Yaakov divided his household into two camps when he prepared to go to war with his brother, Eisov, Bereisheit 32.8

Yaakov faces serious difficulty when his daughter, Deenah, is kidnapped, defiled and held hostage. See Bereisheit 34

Yaakov faces great difficulty when Shimon / Simon and Levi / Levy attacked and killed the men and adult women of Shechem. See Bereisheit 34.7-31. Men from Sh'chem escaped from Shimon and Levi's wrath. They fled to the town of Tapuach and reported their version of what happened to king Yishvi. He sent messengers to all the Emorite kings who in turn drafted tens of thousands of men for battle against Yaakov and his family... Sefer HaYashar (Hoboken, NJ: KTAV Publishing House, Inc., 1993) pp 91 - 94; Rabbi Moshe Weissman, The Midrash Says (Brooklyn, New York: Benei Yakov Publications 1980), pp 326 - 331

Yaakov faces serious pain when Rochel / Rachel dies in childbirth.
See Bereisheit 35.16-20.

Yaakov endures hardship when his oldest son, Reuvein / Ruben enters his bedroom and moves his bed. See Bereisheit 35.22

Mysterious Signs Of The Torah Revealed In GENESIS

Yaakov suffers when his father, Yitzchok dies.
See Bereisheit 35.28,29.

Yaakov endures the hardship of what he thought was Yoseif murder. See Bereisheit 37.18-35

Yaakov faces the hardship of famine.
See Bereisheit 41.56 - 42.1;43.1

Yaakov faces the sorrow of leaving Eretz Canaan for Mitzriam.
See Bereisheit 46.1, 7, 28-31

There is an important point to listing some of Yaakov's disappointments. Yaakov was a righteous man. Yaakov was one of the three patriarchs. Yaakov lived, yet he lived with adversary. Many times our Creator came to Yaakov's rescue yet Yaakov lived with adversity. God, Please help us all!

Our father Yaakov faced adversity. He endured through all the adversity. This being the situation we should ask how did he do this. The answer is Yaakov lived! How did Yaakov live through all this adversity? As stated earlier, Yaakov had a special peace about himself. Yaakov had a special place of peace within himself that he with drew to for renewal and to receive encouragement, strength, guidance and assistance. One could say that Yaakov lived within a protected place. This protective place is revealed to us in Bereisheit 35.7 where Ha Torah says, וַיִּקְרָא לַמָּקוֹם and he called to [the] place אֵל בֵּית־אֵל God is [the] House of God, i.e. There is a Spiritual place which is called the House of God. God dwells there. It is a Spiritual place. It is not a physical house.

Hay Eer {to illuminate / to light}

Lah Maw Kohm {to the place}

216 = 40 ם 6 ו 100 ק 40 מ 30 ל

Yet even though Ha Torah credits Yaakov, Yoseif also lived amidst great adversity. We observe this in two ways.

First, Vayechi {lived} refers to both Yaakov and to Yoseif. Yoseif was seventeen when sold into slavery, Bereisheit 37.2. That means Yoseif lived all but seventeen years of his life in the land of Mitzriam. Yaakov lived in the land of Mitzriam, which would become the land of slavery, for seventeen years,

Mysterious Signs Of The Torah Revealed In GENESIS

Bereisheit 47.9,28.

Vayechi {Lived}

34 = 10 י 8 ח 10 י 6 ו

34 = Yaakov lived 17 years in Mitzriam, Yoseif lived 17 outside of Mitzriam. Together they represent 34.

Twenty-one times in Tenach the letter Lamid precedes the word Ha Ohr {to illuminate / to light}. In other words, the Lamid leads the way to illumination... to light. Yoseif is the one who HaShem sends to Mitzriam first. Yoseif's light shines brightly out of Mitzriam like a beacon. Why? HaShem gave the illumination to Yoseif regarding Pharaoh's dream... regarding proactively preparing for the coming famine. The Gematria of Lamid is 30. The Lamid represents Yoseif. The Lamid represents Yoseif's age when he stood before Pharaoh, Bereisheit 41.46. The Lamid represents the actual years of B'nei Yisroel's living in Mitzriam as 210 {7 x 30} leading up to HaShem's deliverance in Shemot. Rashi states that B'nei Yisroel {excluding Yoseif} spent 210 years in Mitzriam. This is based upon the fact that Yocheved, a daughter of Levi, was 130 years of age when Moshe was born. She was the one recorded in Tenach as born 'between the walls.' Moshe was 80 when HaShem delivered B'nei Yisroel from Mitzriam. {210 = 130 + 80}

So we see through this that Yoseif was the one sent to prepare the way for the survival of his family. Dear one, this may be your destiny in life. Maybe HaShem will use you to bring back those that you love to God. Maybe HaShem will choose you to be the one to return to an observant life in advance of other family members. You may be disowned like Yoseif. You may be sold into slavery. You may suffer for a while. Your resources may be limited for a while. You may lose your position, business, place of employment, family home and even your children for a while. If this were to happen, God Forbid, try to take Yaakov and Yoseif's directive. WE MUST LEARN TO CONTINUE LIVING!

Yoseif and Yaakov are our examples of how to live. Both left home with nothing. Both were separated from those they loved. Both became wealthy over 22 years. Thank God! When we face adversity lets try to live as best as we can like Yaakov and his son, Yoseif. May HaShem be blessed forever!

Dear readers, when so much does not go the way we desire we must learn how to live with adversity!

Mysterious Signs Of The Torah Revealed In GENESIS

The Seven Laws
Chapter 13

Bereisheit 2.16
Bereisheit / Genesis 2.16

Bereisheit 2.16

וַיְצַו יְהוָה אֱלֹהִים עַל־הָאָדָם לֵאמֹר
מִכֹּל עֵץ־הַגָּן אָכֹל תֹּאכֵל:

Bereisheit 2.17

וּמֵעֵץ הַדַּעַת טוֹב וָרָע לֹא תֹאכַל מִמֶּנּוּ
כִּי בְּיוֹם אֲכָלְךָ מִמֶּנּוּ מוֹת תָּמוּת:

And He, HaShem God Commanded to Ha Adam [before they were separated] from all the trees in the garden you may eat freely, Bereisheit 2.16.

And from the Tree of Knowledge of Good and of Evil, do not eat from it. For on the day you eat from it you will certainly die, Bereisheit 2.17

Mysterious Signs Of The Torah Revealed In GENESIS

At the beginning of creation our Creator taught Seven Laws to Adam and Eve. All humanity are required to observe these Commands of our Creator. The Seven Commandments are the foundations of all human and moral progress. They recognize that moral progress and its concomitant Divine love and approval are the privilege and obligation of all mankind.

Commandment One:
Establish and Follow A System of Rulership / Justice

Commandment Two:
Do Not Blaspheme God's Holy Name

Commandment Three:
Only Worship the Creator. Idolatry Is Prohibited.

Commandment Four:
Do Not Murder! Do Not Shed blood!

Commandment Five:
Do Not Take Another Man's Wife Do Not Commit Adultery!

Commandment Six:
Do Not Steal!

Commandment Seven:
Be Kind To Animals!

Mysterious Signs Of The Torah Revealed In GENESIS

I discuss the Seven Laws in more detail in my book, What Does God Require?

Law One: ויצו Vah Yih Tzahv
And He Commanded = {Institute, Law, Order} There is One Who Commands and there are those who receive His Commands. The One Who Commands is Higher... The Creator is in Charge... The Creator is Above those who are Commanded.

Law Two: יהוה HaShem
HaShem = {Prohibition against blasphemy} Dovid Ha Melech said, *'And they shall praise everything from Aleph To Tav of the Name of HaShem for His Name alone is Exalted.'* Tehillim 148:13 The presence of HaShem's Name in written form, in spoken form or in thought form is to be exalted. Any awareness of His Name is to be exalted!! This is necessary because of the Very Holy Essence of His Name. HaShem's Name is unlike any other name. Ha Torah says,

וְלֹא תְחַלְּלוּ אֶת־שֵׁם קָדְשִׁי וְנִקְדַּשְׁתִּי בְּתוֹךְ בְּנֵי יִשְׂרָאֵל אֲנִי יְהוָה מְקַדִּשְׁכֶם :

'And you shall not profane, make common

anything from Aleph to Tav of My Holy Name and I will be sanctified among B'nei Yisroel. I am HaShem who makes you holy.' Vayikra / Leviticus 22.32

Law Three: אלהים El-Heem
God = {Prohibition against idolatry} Anytime we read the word Elokim as we do here we are reminded that this Name is in reference to God our Creator and Judge. We are also reminded that when the exact same word is used with a small e for elohim it is in reference to gods with a small g. Understanding what this means is not complicated. Ha Torah says, *You must not have other gods before My Essence.* Shemot /Exodus 20.3 So when Ha Torah uses the Name Elokim as it does here we are reminded to be careful not to serve other gods. We are reminded of the prohibition of idolatry.

Law Four: עלע–האדם Ahl - Haw Aw Dawm
to the Adam = {Prohibition against bloodshed} Here the words Ahl {on, upon, over, against} represent the prohibition of blood shed. When the Creator Appoints us to be over 'the man' it has the impact of protecting or guarding the man. On the other hand the last two letters of Adam represent dom {blood} so one could say the Creator prohibits the shedding of blood.

Mysterious Signs Of The Torah Revealed In GENESIS

Law Five: לאמר - Lay Mor

Saying = {Prohibition against adultery} This represents the **Law** proper sequence of events. A father and mother of the same beliefs and observances have the responsibility of passing on to their children utterances, sayings and words of Ha Torah. So when Ha Torah says Lay Mohr it is in reference to to the necessary sequence of proper events required to pass an utterance of Ha Torah on. In other words one must get married to an individual of the same belief with the same goals and ideals. They must have children. They must raise their children in observance of Ha Torah. When these conditions exist then and only then is it possible to pass on utterances of Ha Torah. There is no Spiritual adultery or physical adultery.

Law Six: מכל עץ הגן Mee Cawl - Aytz - Ha Gawn

From all of the trees = {Prohibition against stealing} Mee Cawl - Aytz - Ha Gawn represents that Adam and Chava could eat from every tree in Gan Eden but one. They were prohibited from eating from the Tree of Knowledge of Good and Evil. When we take what is prohibited from us that action is stealing.

Law Seven: אצל תאצל Aw Chohl - Toh Chohl

Eat freely = {Be kind to animals} represented to Adam

and Chava that they could eat freely of all plant life except the Tree of Knowledge of Good and Evil. This meant they could not eat animals. Later to Noach and his descendants this meant one was required to not remove limbs from a living animals and eat them. Ha Torah considers such an action immoral and unkind to animals. The point is that one must take the kindest and most gentle approach to taking an animals life.

Additional Information
There is a wealth of additional information like the following two examples that prove the existence of the Seven Noach Commandments.

In addition to the Seven Noach Commandments, history proves some information on several other forms of justice existing thousands of years back. Consider the Hammurabi Code and the Assyrian Laws which are both in excess of 3,800 years old and the Hittite Code which descended from Heth the great grandson of Noach. Each of these are shorter versions of the Seven Noach Commandments.

It is the Seven Laws that the people of Nineveh returned to and embraced that prevented their destruction.

Mysterious Signs Of The Torah Revealed In GENESIS

Glossary Index

Abraham - aka Avraham #85 and Avram - See Genesis 17.5 [Avraham ben Terach] - means *'Father of Nations'*.

Abram - aka Avram #87 - See Genesis 11.26

Abimelech - Avimelech #40 king of Gerar - means *'Father of king'*

Adam - aka [הָאָדָם] Ha Adam, Adam #120 Ha Reshon Adam #120 - meaning - *'man, the man, men, humankind'*.

Akeidah - The Akeidah עקדה - See Genesis 22 - See The Schottenstein Edition Siddur for Weekdays With An Interlinear Translation) - The Akeidah is a prayer in a Jewish Siddur which is prayed everyday. - means *'the binding, the self sacrifice'*

Aleph - [א] The Aleph #502 - #507 is the first letter of the Hebrew Aleph Bet / Hebrew Alpha Bet. The Aleph = One. The Aleph is representative of HaShem / the L-rd. The Aleph means - *'to learn, to train, one thousand'*.

Mysterious Signs Of The Torah Revealed In GENESIS

Aleph Bet - means *'the Hebrew Alphabet'.*

Aleph to Tav - [א ת] When I use the words 'from Aleph to Tav,' I mean 'from the first Letter of the Aleph Bet, the Letter Aleph [א] to the last Letter of the Aleph Bet, the Letter Tav [ת].' The Eht represents being all inclusive from the beginning of one letter to the conclusion of another letter. *'The word Et is spelled Alef Tav, the first and last letters of the Hebrew alphabet. It therefore implies a transition from beginning to end. Rabbi Ishmael therefore states that its main purpose [in the instance he is referring to] is to indicate the transitive sense of the word "created."*

Rabbi Akiba, on the other hand replies that the very fact that Et contains the Alef Tav implies that it superimposes the entire alphabet between the subject verb and the predicated noun adding all things that pertain to that noun(Cf. Or Torah, Bereisheit). See <u>The Bahir</u> p p 108, 109

Amorah - Ha Torah Says, [עַל־סְדֹם וְעַל־עֲמֹרָה] 'On Sedom and on Amorah. <u>The KJV</u> says, *'upon Sodom and upon Go-morrah'*. However there is no [ג] Letter Gimmel which is the only Hebrew letter that

Mysterious Signs Of The Torah Revealed In GENESIS

has the 'G' sound.

Angel - See Malach - Angel #4397 means *'messenger.'*

Ark - Ark # 8392 means *'a box, a chest'*

Avram - See Abraham.

Avraham - See Abraham

Aveinu - [אבינו] means *'our father'*.

Babel - Bavel or Babylon #894. See Genesis 10.10; 11.9 - It was in Babylon where one language, Hebrew, was confused into seventy languages.

Bayit - Bayit #1004 means *'house'*.

Bereisheit - [בְּרֵאשִׁית] is the Hebrew name for Genesis. Bereisheit is the first word of Ha Torah. Bereisheit is the first book of Ha Torah. There are fifty chapters in Bereisheit. Bereisheit means *'in the beginning'*.

Bereisheit Bereisheit - Genesis 1.1 - 6.8
This is the first Parshat of twelve within the book of

Mysterious Signs Of The Torah Revealed In GENESIS

Genesis. Bereisheit means beginnings. When Bereisheit is repeated its *'Great beginnings'*.

Bereisheit Chayei Sarah - Genesis 23.1 - 25.18
This is the fifth Parshat of twelve within the book of Genesis. Chayei Sarah means *'the life of Sarah.'*

Bereisheit Noach - Genesis 6.9 - 11.32
This is the second Parshat of twelve within the book of Genesis. Noach is the Noah of the flood. Noach means *'restful.'*

Bereisheit Lech Lecha - Genesis 12.1 -17.27
This is the third Parshat of twelve within the book of Genesis. Lech Lecha means *'Go! Get out!'*

Bereisheit Mikeitz - Genesis 41.1 - 44.17
This is the tenth Parshat of twelve within the book of Genesis. Mikeitz means *'at the end.'*

Bereisheit Toldot - Genesis 25.19 - 28.9
This is the sixth Parshat of twelve within the book of Genesis. Toldot means *'history or generations'*.

Bereisheit Vayechi - Genesis 47.28 - 50.26
This is the twelfth Parshat of twelve within the book of Genesis. Vayechi means *'and he lived'*.

Mysterious Signs Of The Torah Revealed In GENESIS

Bereisheit Vayeishev - Bereisheit / Genesis 37.1 – 40.23 This is the ninth Parshat of twelve within the book of Genesis. Vayeishev means *'and he settled'*.

Bereisheit Vayeitzei - Genesis 28.10 - 32.3
This is the seventh Parshat of twelve within the book of Genesis. Vayeitzei means *'and he left'*.

Bereisheit Vayera - Genesis 18.1 -22.24
This is the fourth Parshat of twelve within the book of Genesis. Vayera means *'and He Appeared'*.

Bereisheit Vayigash - Genesis 44.18 - 47.27
This is the eleventh Parshat of twelve within the book of Genesis. Vayigash means *'and he approached.'*

Bereisheit Vayishlach - Genesis 32.4 - 36.43
This is the eight Parshat of twelve within the book of Genesis. Vayishlach means *'and he sent'*.

Bet - [ב] is the second letter of the Hebrew Aleph Bet. Bet #1004 - #1006 means *'house'*.

Bilhah - See Genesis 29.29 Bilhah #1090 means *'terror, disaster, calamity troubled'*.

Mysterious Signs Of The Torah Revealed In GENESIS

B'nei Yisroel - [בְּנֵי־יִשְׂרָאֵל] - See Genesis 32.33 {He}; Genesis 32.32 Bnei Yisroel means *'children of Israel'*.

B'nai Noachides - B'nai Noach [בְּנֵי־נֹחַ] See Genesis 18.9 means *'the sons / children of Noach'*.

Brit Milah - [בְּרִית מִילָה] is the ritual circumcision. Brit #1285 [בְּרִית] means 'covenant'. Milah #4139 [מִילָה] means 'circumcision'.

Cain - aka Kayin [He]; Cain - Cain is the first son of Adam and Chavah / Eve. See Genesis 4.1

Canaan - Canaan #3667 [כְּנָעַן] is the land of Israel. Canaan means *'merchant, merchandise trader'*.

Chanoch - aka Enoch- Chanoch [He]; Enoch #2585 is the father of Methushelach [He]; Methuselah means *'education or training'*. However there is no Letter [א] Aleph or Letter [ע] Ayin which are the only Hebrew letters that have the 'Ee' sound.

Charan - is a city in northwestern Mesopotamia, just east of the Euphrates River. It is normally a seventeen day journey from Chevron. See <u>The Midrash Says</u> p 217.

Mysterious Signs Of The Torah Revealed In GENESIS

Chavah - aka Chavah [He]; Eve #2332 - There is no Letter [א] Aleph or Letter [ע] Ayin which are the only Hebrew letters that have the 'Ee' sound. Chavah means - *'life, living'*.

Chief Baker - *'officer over bakery'*.

Chief Butler *'officer over butlers'*.

Chief Executioner - [שַׂר הַטַּבָּחִים] *'officer over executions'*.

Chof [כ] is the eleventh Letter of the Aleph Bet. Chof means *'spoon'* or the *'palm'* of ones hand.

Commandment - [צוה] See Mitzvah Command, Commanded and Commandment #6680 come from the same root. Commandment is an 'order'.

Creator - Creator is a name I like to use for HaShem God, the L-rd God.

Deenah - Deenah [He] Dinah # 1783 is the first daughter of Yaakov and Leah. See Genesis 30.21 Deenah means *'judgment'*.
Divine - I use Divine to mean from or of God. Divine

can mean holy as in the Holy Scriptures.

Dream - Dreams # 2472 recorded in Ha Torah are prophetic.

Egypt - aka [מִצְרַיִם] Mitzrim {He} Egypt #4714 . This is the country that gave birth to B'nei Yisroel. Mitzrim is at the northeastern part of Africa, next to Palestine. Mitzrim means *'heavy darkness, gloom'*.

Elifaz - [אלפז] is the son of Eisov and Grandson of Yitzchok and nephew of Yaakov.

Emeinu - [אמנו] means *'our mother'*.

Erev Shabbat - [ערב שבת] This is Yom Shi Shi / the sixth day in the evening, It is Friday evening.

Eisov - aka Eisov [He]; Esau # 6215 means *'hairy'*.

Eretz Canaan - [אֶרֶץ כְּנַעַן] aka Eretz Canaan [He]; the land of Canaan
Esav - See Eisov

Evier - aka Evier [He]; Eber #5677 is the great grandson of Shem ben Noach, the son of Noach. Shem and Eiver established a school / Yeshiva where Avraham, Yitzchok and Yaakov learned. Evier means *'to Hebraize, to [teach[the Jewish religion culture]'*.

Fo'c'sle - This is the extreme forward compartment of a ship.

Flood - When Ha Tenach speaks about a flood #3999 it is reference to the flood in Noach's time. The flood began in 1656 CF [from Creation]. See Dr. Akiva Gamliel's 16 month calendar.

Gabriel - This is in reference to the Malach / Angel Gabriel #1403 whose name means *'God of strength'* [He] or *'Man of God* . See Bava Metzia 86b - n (37)

Gematria - This is a systematic method of revealing and understanding Biblical exegesis through the relationship of Hebrew letters and numbers. Gematria applies to the Torah, Tenach, Prayer Siddurim and other such books. The origin is not Hebrew but possibly from Greek 'Geometria'
Gargantuan - Very large task.

Gematria Miluy - means *'each Letter of a Letter Hebrew Aleph Bet is spelled out.'*
Gomorrah - See Amorah

Mysterious Signs Of The Torah Revealed In GENESIS

Ha Adam - See Ha Reshon - Adam #120

Hagar - Hagar #1904 was the daughter of Pharaoh, a Princess who was given to Sarah as a servant because of his miss deeds. Pharaoh tried to take Sarah for his wife when she was already married to Avraham. Hagar became the wife of Avraham. She bore Avraham a son, Yishmael. Later Sarah told Avraham to *'Drive out this slave woman and her son...'* Genesis 21.10. Later after Sarah's death Avraham took Hagar back as his wife. Hagar's name was changed to Keturah. See the Artscroll Tanach Series, Bereisheit Vol 1 pp 965, 966

Ha Mikdosh - [בית מקדש קדוש] means the *'Holy Temple'*.

Ha Reshon - When one carefully examines Ha Torah they will notice that the original reference to [הָאָדָם] Ha Adam was to both Adam the first man and Chavah / Eve the first lady. See Genesis 1.27. They shared the same body known as Ha Adam. See Genesis 1.26, 27; Genesis 5.1, 2 *'This is the Book of Generations / Histories of humankind in the day God Created [singular] Adam [singular]. With male parts and female parts He created them [in one body].* He blessed them and named them

[Adam]. on the day they were Created.' See The Metsudah Chumash / Rashi p 54; See The Midrash Says p 33

Ha Reshon means *'the first man'*.

Ha Reshonah - means *'the first lady'*.

HaShem - Ha means *'the'* and Shem means *'Name'*.

Hevel - aka Hevel [He]; Abel #1893 was the brother that was the first human being on earth to be murdered. Hevel was murdered by his brother Kayin. See Genesis 4.8. There is no Letter [א] Aleph or Letter [ע] Ayin in Hevel. These are the only Hebrew letters that have the 'Ah' sound. Hevel means *'emptiness, breath, steam'*.

Horticulture - is the art or practicing garden cultivation

Isaac - aka Yitzchok [He]; Isaac #3327 See Yitzchok Isaac means *'laughter'*.

Jordan River - aka [נהר הירדן] Nehar Ha Yarden is a river in southwest Asia that flows 251 kilometers / 156 miles and ending at the Dead Sea.

Judaism - observes the 613 mitzvot of ha Torah.

Mysterious Signs Of The Torah Revealed In GENESIS

Kal Yisroel - means *'all of Israel'*.

Katan - means *'smaller'*.

Kayin - aka Kayin [He]; Cain - Kayin is the first son of Adam and Chavah / Eve. See Genesis 4.1

KJV - King James Authorized Version of the Bible 1611.

Kohein - aka Kohen - A descendant of Aharon the Kohen Gadol / High Priest. The Kohein was responsible for performing duties in the Holy Temple.

Kohen Gadol - High Priest. There is only one high priest at a time.

Levi - Levi #3878 is the third son of Yaakov and Leah. See Genesis 29.34

Lot - The nephew of Avraham. Lot #3876 means *'to wrap, to cover'*.

Malach - See Angel #4397 - Malach means *'messenger.'*

Malki Tzedek - means *'King of Righteousness'* is Shem the son of Noach. After the flood he was known as the king of peace and righteousness.

Mem - [מ] The Letter Mem is the thirteenth Letter of the Hebrew Aleph Bet. The Mem is used to define *'comparative thought'*.

Menasheh - aka Menasheh [He]; Manasseh #4519

Methushelach - aka Mesushelach [He]; Methuselah # 4968 [מתושלח] [מת] death [ו] and [שלח] to send - Methushelach means *'[when this child] dies send death'*.

Milkah - aka Milkah [He]; Milcah #4435 ; was the mother of Rivkah / Rebekah. Milkah means *'the queen'*.
Mishlei - [משלי] is the Book of Proverbs

Mispar Katan - is where ONLY the first number is counted. For examples: 10 is 1, 100 is 1, 90 is 9, 60 is 6 and 400 is 4.

Mitzvah - [צוה] Command, Commanded and Commandment #6680 come from the same root. Commandment is an 'order'.
Mitzvot - See Mitzvah - means *'Command'*.

Mysterious Signs Of The Torah Revealed In GENESIS

Mitzraim - See Egypt

Mysticism - Jewish Mysticism is and integral part of the Chassidic movement within Judaism. The mystical school of thought known as Kabbalah. Mysticism explains many things not understood. Mysticism opens the door to esoteric thought.

Mystical - Mystical relates to mystics of Jewish though who study allegory and symbols transcending human understanding.

Mystically - See Mystical

Neshamah - [נשמה] Neshamah is the third level of the soul. Neshamah means 'Spirit Mind'. This is the intellect that permits us to connect with Creator. [רוח] Ruach is the second level of the soul. Ruach has mortal virtues and distinguishes between good and evil. [נפש] Nefesh the first level of the soul. The Nefesh is our animal like instincts and cravings.
[חיה] Chayyah is the soul that opens our awareness of the Divine life force. [יחידה] Yehidah is the fifth level of the soul that has the ability to unity with the Creator.

Noach - aka Noach [He], Noah #5146 - means 'rest'.

Mysterious Signs Of The Torah Revealed In GENESIS

Osnat - aka Osnat [He] Asenath # 621 is the daughter of Deenah who was assaulted by Shechem. She is the grand daughter of Yaakov and the daughter in law of Yaakov. As a child Osnat was driven from Yaakov's house by her uncles according to Pirkei d'Rabbi Eliezer. This was because her uncles were concerned that people would speak of licentiousness in their tents. They were concerned that people would think that they were morally perverse. Yaakov engraved a metal plate and put it around her neck. The words stated that whoever married her would be marrying a relative of Yaakov's family. Osnat was placed under a bush. A Malach took her to the house of Potifer in Mitzriam. His wife, Zulaicha raised her as their own daughter. Twenty-two years later Pharaoh ordered that Osnat marry Yoseif. See Artscroll Bereisheit Vol 2 pp 1800, 1801.

Passuk - means *'verse'*.

Pharaoh - Pharaoh # 6547 means *'great house'*.

Pirkei d'Rabbi Eliezer - This is a Tannaitic midrashic book written by Rabbi Eliezer ben Hyrcanus.

Mysterious Signs Of The Torah Revealed In GENESIS

Potiphar - aka Poti-phera, Potipherah #6319 was the step father in law of Yoseif. See Genesis 41.50

Potifer's Wife - See Zulaicha

Rachel - Rachel [He] Rachel #7354 means *'ewe, sheep'*.

Raphael - [רפאל]means *'Angel of healing'*. Bava Metzia 86b -n (360

Rashi - Simon ben Isaac, a French rabbinical scholar 1040 -1105.

Raw Shaw - means *'evil'*.

Reuvein - aka Reuvein [He], Reuben #7205 is the first son of Yaakov and Leah. See Genesis 29.32

Rivkah - aka Rivkah [He], Rebekah #7259 means *'team'*.

Rosh Hashanah - [ראש השנה] Rosh Hashanah is the birthday of the world. It is the day all created things stand in judgment before their Creator. Rosh Hashanah means *'head of the year'*.

Mysterious Signs Of The Torah Revealed In GENESIS

Sabbath - [שבת] Sabbath [He] Sabbath #7676 is the seventh day of the week. B'nei Yisroel is commanded to rest on the seventh day. Sabbath mean *'to rest, to cease from labor'*.

Samech - [ס] The Letter Samech is the fifteenth Letter of the Hebrew Aleph Bet. Samech means *'support, i.e. One can be relied upon.'*

Sarah - aka Sarah or Sarai was the wife of Avraham. See Genesis 11.29 and Genesis 17.15. Sarah #8283 means *'a noble woman, a Minister'*.

Shechem - Shechem #7927 is a name for the prince of Shechem who assaulted Deenah, daughter of Yaakov. Shechem means *'back, shoulder'*.

School of Shem and Evier - See Evier

Sefer Ha Yonah - means *'The Book of Jonah'*.

Seven Commands - originate from Bereisheit 2.16. The Seven Commands were given to Adam and Chavah / Eve to observe.

Seven Laws - See Seven Commands

Mysterious Signs Of The Torah Revealed In GENESIS

Seventy Languages - See Genesis 10.10; 11.9 - It was in Babylon where one language, Hebrew, was confused into seventy languages.

Shechinah - is the *'Presence of the Alm-ghty'*.

Shem - Shem #8035 was a son of Noach. Shem means *'name'*.

Shema Yisroel - [שְׁמַע יִשְׂרָאֵל] means *'Hear Oh Israel'*. See Deuteronomy 6.4 - 9

Shimon - aka Shimon [He], Simeon #8095 is the second son of Yaakov and Leah. See Genesis 29.33 Simeon means *'heard'*.

Shlomo Ha Melech - aka Shlomo Ha Melech [He], king Solomon #8010 *'Solomon'* means *'peace'*.

Spirituality is one who is a Spiritual person, i.e they observe the Seven Laws of the Bible.

Spiritualist / Noachide Covenant - This was given to Noach after the flood. See Genesis 9.8 - 17

Sodom - Sodom #5467 is the city that Avraham's nephew, Lot lived in that was destroyed by fire from heaven. See Genesis 19.24.

Taryag Mitzvot - [תריג מצות] are the 613 Commands from Ha Torah given to the B'nei Yisroel.

Tav - [ת] is the twenty second letter i.e the last letter of the Hebrew Aleph Bet. Tav means *'sign, mark'*.

Tehillim - [תהלים] Tehillim is the Hebrew word for the Book of Psalms. Tehillim means *'psalms'*.

Tenach - [תנ"ך] aka Tenach, Tanach or Tanakh is an acronym that identifies

[תורה נביאים כתובים] The acronym represents: the Writings [ך] the Prophets [נ] the Torah [ת]. Christians refer to Ha Tenach as the Old Testament.

Terach - means *'imbecile'*.

Torah -[תורה] is Genesis {Bereisheit}, Exodus {Shemot}, Leviticus {Vayikra}, Numbers {Bamidbar} and Deuteronomy {Devarim} are the five Books of Ha Torah. The Five Books of Moshe {Moses} and the Pentateuch are other names for Ha Torah. The books of Ha Torah were given to Moshe on Har Sinai by God. In addition to the Torah, the Written Law, God Gave Moshe a more comprehensive explanation of the Written Law known as the Oral Law; both the Written and Oral Law constitute the Torah. Torah means *'Law'*.

Tzaddik - means *'righteous'*

Ur Kasdim - is defined by our sages as the fiery furnaces of Chaldee. See the <u>Artscroll Tanach Series, Bereisheit</u> Vol 1 348, 349; 515

Viceroy - One who rules on behalf of a sovereign.
Yaakov - aka Yaakov [He], Jacob #3290 is the son of Yitzchok and grandson of Avraham. See Genesis 25.26. Yaakov means *'grip his heel'*.

Yardon River - See Jordan River

Yay Tzehr Raw - means *'evil inclination'*.

Yay Tzehr Tov - means *'good inclination'*.

Yehudah - aka Yehudah [He], Judah #3063 is the fourth son of Yaakov and Leah. See Genesis 29.35 Yehudah means *'praise'*.

Yerushalayim - aka Yerushalayim [He], Jerusalem #

Mysterious Signs Of The Torah Revealed In GENESIS

3389 means *'to teach peace'*.

Yishmael - aka Yishmael [He], Ishmael #3458 means *'He, God will hear'*.

Yitzchok - aka Yitzchok [He]; Isaac #3327 Yitzchok is the son of Avraham and Sarah and the father of Yaakov. See Yitzchok Isaac means *'laughter'*.

Yom Kippur - means *'day of atonement'*.

Yoseif - aka Yoseif [He], Joseph #3130 is the eleventh son of Yaakov and the first son of Rochel. See Genesis 30.25 Yoseif means *'HaShem added'*.

Yud - [י] The Letter Yud is the tenth Letter of the Hebrew Aleph Bet. Yud means *'a jot.'*

Zayin - [ז] The Letter Zayin is the seventh Letter of the Aleph Bet. Zayin means *'arms'* or *'weapon'*.

Zulaicha - Foster mother of Osnat. Wife of Potifer.

Mysterious Signs Of The Torah Revealed In GENESIS

Mysterious Signs Of The Torah Revealed In GENESIS

Torah References

Bereisheit Genesis		Bereisheit Genesis		Bereisheit Genesis	
Ref.	Page	Ref.	Page	Ref.	Page
1.3	25	4.9-16	71	17.1-22	73
1.4	21	6.13-21	73	17.5	143
1.4	22 / 23	7.1	29	17.9	89
1.28-30	70	7.1-4	73	17.17	60
		7.16	73	17.18-21	89
		8.15	73	18.1-33	73
2.2,3		9.1-17	73	18.15	74
2.3	86	11.7-9	73	19.1-29	75
2.4	85	11.26	142	20.3-8	75
2.2-4	84	11.31	40	21.5	44
2.15-17	70	12.1	37	21.5	44
2.15,16	137	12.1	39	21.8	73
2.16	25/137	12.1	77	21.12	56
		12.1-3	73	21.17-21	60/75
		12.7,8	73	22	75
2.20-22	70	12.14-17	73	22.1	47
3.9-24	70	14.18	87	22.1,2	73
3.13-16	70	15.1	95	22.11-24	73
4.7	58	15.1-20	73	23.1	53/60/62
4.6,7	71	16.7	75	23.1	146

Mysterious Signs Of The Torah Revealed In GENESIS

Bereisheit Genesis		Bereisheit Genesis		Yishaiah Isaiah	
Ref.	Page	Ref.	Page	Ref.	Page
24.16	62	30.36	63	35.22	132
24.57	62	31.1	131	35.28	88
25.7	88	31.3	69	37.2	60
25.16	62	31.3	77	37.7	113
25.21	62	31.41	63/78	39.2	91
25.21	130	31.41	79	40.16	114
25.22,23	61	32.8	132	40.16,17	115
25.23	74	32.11	79	41.12	118
25.26	62	32.26-33	131	41.16	119
25.29-34	130	32.41	79	41.29	77
26.2-5	75	34	132	41.39	118
26.34 -	130	34.7-31	132	41.39	120
26.35	130	35.28,29	88/133	41.39	117
26.34-36	131	35.29	133	41.41	93
27.1	131	35.7	113/134	41.45	103
27.41	68	35.7	128/129	41.46	77
28.12-15	75	35.16-22	132	41.46	90
29.18-30	131	37.18-35	133	41.56	133/135
30.25-26	78	37.2	60/134	41.46	135
30.35	63	35.16-20	132	42.1-43.1	134

Mysterious Signs Of The Torah Revealed In GENESIS

Bereisheit Genesis		Bereisheit Genesis		Yishaiah Isaiah	
Ref.	Page	Ref.	Page	Ref.	Page
43.1	134	50.26	88	40.31	59
45.6	77	50.26	110		
45.18	122	50.26	123/146		
45.19	111				
46.1	134			Tehillim Psalms	
46.6	115				
46.6	115	Shemot Exodus		Ref.	Page
46.7	134			19.8	17
46.28-31	134	Ref.	Page	91.1,4	35
47.9	77	20.3	140	145.18,19	27
47.9	129	20.12	17	148.13	137
47.28	88				
47.28	123	Vaylkra Leviticus		Mishlei Proverbs	
47.28	124				
47.28	88	Ref.	Page	Ref.	Page
47.28	123/146	22.32	140	31.10	54
50.5,6	99	Devarim Deuteronomy		31.31	58
50.7	100				
50.22	60	Ref.	Page		
32.11	59	32.11	59		

Mysterious Signs Of The Torah Revealed In GENESIS

ABOUT THE AUTHOR

Dr. Akiva Gamliel Belk

Our Sages Teach that one should run from Honor. I am a Ba'al Teshuvah, a Jew who has returned to Judaism. I am deeply grateful for those who supported Jewish outreach to assist Jews like me in returning to Torah Observance. I do not feel like a great man, but instead, a man who will stand before the Creator of everything in the universe and give account of my actions. My degrees will not stand before the Creator. I will stand before the Creator. I will be welcomed into His Presence not because I believe in Jesus but because: God Loves me and has forgiven every sin, even my blatant rebellious sins… because I acknowledge my sin before God and make a plan to turn away from that sin and make it right for my errors… because I try to Observe His Commands in the Torah. The Lord our God is

Mysterious Signs Of The Torah Revealed In GENESIS

gracious.

www.ingramcontent.com/pod-product-compliance
Lightning Source LLC
Chambersburg PA
CBHW071716090426
42738CB00009B/1794